D1124577

To:

_____

From:

_____

$\mathcal{S}$ing and make music in your
heart to the Lord, always
giving thanks to God the
Father for everything.

—EPHESIANS 5:19–20

Simple Gifts: Unwrapping the Special Moments of Everyday Life
Copyright 1999 by New Life Clinics

ISBN 0-310-97811-4

Requests for information should be addressed to:
    Inspirio, the Gift Group of Zondervan
    Grand Rapids, Michigan 49530

Senior editor: Gwen Ellis
Project editor: Kathyrn Yanni
Designer: John Lucas

Printed in China

01 02 03 /HK/ 9 8

SIMPLE GIFTS

*Unwrapping the
Special Moments
of Everyday Life*

inspirio

The gift group of Zondervan

Contents

Remember What Matters

Patsy Clairmont

When I think of simple pleasures, I think of chasing sunsets on my nifty bicycle in the desert of California, where we winter. The sunsets slather the mountains in mounds of scrumptious peachy colors, and I love to ride my electric-blue bike in pursuit of the last yummy remnants of the day. (My bike is the comforting, old-fashioned kind with coaster brakes. I damaged my knees on fancy bikes, and now my family doesn't trust me with anything that has controls on the handlebars.) I linger on my bicycle until the sky fades, blanketing the mountains in evening, and then I turn around and pedal for home, satisfied with my colorful pursuit.

Simple joys include deep, cushioned chairs and delicious books. I delight in children's stories like *Emily of New Moon*,

Toot and Puddle, and *The Secret Garden.* I love to feast my eyes on the garden artwork of Marjolein Bastin and the seascapes and field pictures of Winslow Homer. Some evenings I lose myself in a Francine Rivers novel or travel through Mitford with Jan Karon or linger over the deep words of Ken Gire.

Speaking of delicious, reminds me of banana popsicles, a favorite treat of mine. They remind me of my mother's banana cream puddings. She alternated layers of vanilla wafers, cooked pudding, and sliced bananas, topping it with a two-inch layer of meringue, all golden brown at the edges. Yum! The other day my husband came home from the grocery store and said, "I'm sorry, honey; they were all out of banana popsicles." I thought, *How dear of him to remember this little craving, to note that this would please me.*

Hmm, everyday gifts—bikes, books, banana popsicles—truly are often the sweetest—and the easiest to come by.

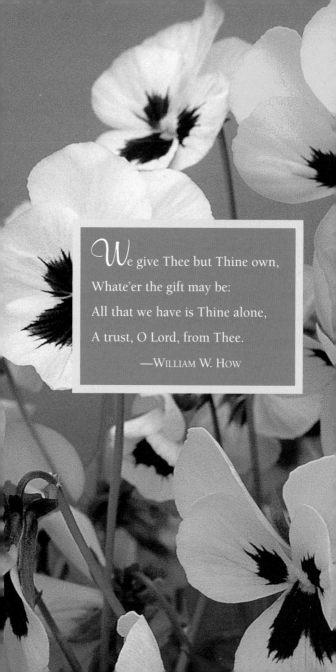

We give Thee but Thine own,
Whate'er the gift may be:
All that we have is Thine alone,
A trust, O Lord, from Thee.

—WILLIAM W. HOW

Come, all you who are thirsty,
  come to the waters;
and you who have no money,
    come, buy and eat!
Come, buy wine and milk
    without money and without
      cost.
Why spend money on what is not
      bread,
    and your labor on what does
      not satisfy?
Listen, listen to me, and eat what
      is good,
    and your soul will delight in
      the richest of fare.

—Isaiah 55:1–2

The Best Things in Life Are Free

$\mathcal{M}$ost people think that the good things in life come with a winning sweepstakes ticket: a new car, a bigger house, a Caribbean cruise. But whoever said, "The best things in life are free" had it right.

I think it's pretty thrilling when I gather an armload of hydrangeas out of my own backyard. I'm in awe when I pluck off a juicy pear and partake of the fruit of the land. And I'm ecstatic when the spring flowers burst forth with shouts of alleluia. I also think it's worth celebrating when I meet a stranger and she offers me a warm smile, or someone extends a helping hand. I remember being in the Dallas–Fort Worth airport one time. I was exhausted, trying to make my way home. As we arrived at the gate, I learned that my next connection was about three cities away. *I will NEVER make it*, I thought.

I saw one of those handicapped carts nearby, and I asked, "Is there any way I could get a ride to my gate?"

"Just a moment and I'll tell you," answered the driver, because she was obligated to take anyone who was handicapped first. When she finished loading priority passengers, there was one spot left. She curled her finger up, motioning for me to come and sit in that spot. I was so grateful that when I sat down, I started to cry.

When you extend a helping hand to someone else, you never know how deeply she may need it. Be on the lookout for life's freebies. Whether you're giving or receiving, they're some of the best bargains around.

This day, Lord: Thank you for the everyday gifts of life. Alert me to opportunities to extend them to others. Amen.

Fuss with the Flowers

One simple pleasure I enjoy is painting tulips with watercolors. I took a watercolor class once with a friend who is very good at art, but she is shy, so I attended the classes to support her. As soon as the class started, I knew I was out of my league, but I did learn how to use the supplies. And once I left the class and was not under any pressure to produce, I even painted some recognizable flowers (previously they had looked like ailing sea creatures). What fun!

I have activities that delighted me in childhood that have carried over into my adult life as well. Fussing with my flowers is a big one. When I was a little girl, I loved to play outside. I found pleasure in the feel of grass under my bare feet, in the fresh breeze on my face, in picking a bouquet of wildflowers.

Now I love to putter in my garden in Michigan, and during the winter I fiddle around with potted flowers at our desert nest. My thoughts flow easily and simply as I tend to my plants, especially around how

God is our Creator and how he tends to us. I am filled with gratitude and awe that he has designed the world with such beauty and detail. The delight of immersing myself in plants and flowers refreshes me in a simple but powerful way.

I chuckle when I get to look into the face of a smiling pansy. I'm so amazed at how God has cleverly, humorously, and beautifully designed this world. Pansies are the chortlers of the garden. Other varieties are joyful and know how to celebrate—the trumpeting lily, for example—but the little pansies, well, are crowded close to the earth giggling their heads off. Sometimes I stick my face down by theirs to be a part of the fun for a moment.

Want simple pleasures? Take time to fuss with the flowers.

This day, Lord: Thank you for the detailed beauty and lovely fragrance of flowers. I rejoice in how they reflect your tenderness and artistry as the Creator.

$\mathcal{G}$od draws up the drops of water,
   which distill as rain to the streams;
the clouds pour down their moisture
   and abundant showers fall on mankind.
Who can understand how he spreads out the
      clouds,
   how he thunders from his pavilion?
See how he scatters his lightning about him,
   bathing the depths of the sea.
This is the way he governs the nations
   and provides food in abundance.
He fills his hands with lightning
   and commands it to strike its mark.
His thunder announces the coming storm;
   even the cattle make known its approach.
At this my heart pounds
   and leaps from its place.

—Job 36:27–37:1

For thee the wonder-working
earth puts forth sweet flowers.
—Lucretius

The Power of Beauty

$\mathcal{M}$y mother was a very creative woman. She could upholster furniture, crochet magnificent floor-length tablecloths, take junk and transform it into treasures, and bring order into chaos. Mom was even creative with finances. My dad was a milk-man, so with a skim-milk budget, Mom couldn't go out and be extravagant. She had a way, however, of rearranging what we already owned in innovative ways. She'd rattle around in cupboards and closets, looking for finds to incorporate; then she'd carry furniture from one room to another and voilà: a new look! I have tried to carry that legacy into our family's home. I too love to arrange things around the house so that wherever you look, there are touches reminiscent of my mom.

One of the loveliest events of my growing-up years was the birth of my sister, when I was thirteen years old. It was pretty thrilling for me at that age to have a baby sister in the house. She replaced my baby doll and was a very important person in my life. I helped take care of her each day; I helped bathe her, feed her, and dress her up. She was so pretty that I just loved showing her off to people. I remember one day when I set up our living room like a studio and took a whole roll of pictures of her in a frilly dress. I was very aware of what a miracle it was to have this new life in our family.

That miracle came back to me when I gave birth to my own baby. I looked at that baby and thought, *This is one of the first right things you've ever produced.* And then I thought, *There must be a God, to make something this beautiful.*

Beauty has great power to soften our hearts and draw us to a deeper awareness of who God is. Don't overlook its healing potential to soothe your spirit in troubled times, to draw you into worship of the One whose beauty is beyond all earthly comparison.

This day, Lord: Thank you for the ways in which beauty focuses the gaze of my heart on you. Give me your creative Spirit for reaching out to others with touches of beauty.

Disown Your Own Stuff

Okay, I confess I have way too much stuff. And the one thing I've learned about stuff is, it will eat up your joy more quickly than anything. For as much fun as it is to accumulate it, somebody has to take care of it. It has to be hemmed, dusted, assembled, adjusted, and fussed over. It always requires something of you. Maintenance, maintenance, maintenance. After a while you begin to realize that less is more.

Every once in a while, my childhood friend of forty years and I would decide to clean up our act by emptying out our stuff. We'd have a race in order to encourage each other to dig under beds, shovel out closets, and bulldoze through garage debris. Then we'd visit each other's stack of stuff to see who won. That was a bad move because then I'd leave with a trunkload of her junk and she'd haul a stack of my stuff into her house. Hmm, something's awry with this system, but we haven't quite fixed it yet. We're working on it, though.

You can see I'm not all that successful at eliminating stuff, but I sure know a lot about how it can consume your time and energy. I think my stuff is pretty well Velcroed to me. At least it's not Super Glued.

Some day I'm going to do something about all my stuff. Successfully. Then I'll write a big book about it. For now I'll have to stick with a few paragraphs and one last line of advice. If you want to enjoy life's simple gifts, be willing to thin out, give away, some of your stuff.

This day, Lord: I want to simplify my life by clearing out unnecessary stuff. Help me to shape my perspective on material things according to your priorities, not mine. Amen.

The Taste of Humble Pie

Humility has been described as the art of living according to the truth of who you are in relationship to yourself, to others, and to God. I remember a time when I was invited to speak at a leadership conference. Initially I felt so honored, because I was such a little squirt, and here I was going to talk to all the big squirts. I thought, *This is great!* But the more I thought about it, the more I yearned to tell these leaders a thing or two. I started to pull out principles and Scriptures that I felt they needed to hear.

The morning of that conference, I woke up and I had my first case of laryngitis. I had no voice. After gargling and gargling, I came up with kind of a raspy croak.

I stepped out into the hall and bumped into one of the big squirts.

He said, "Hi, Patsy!"

I tried to greet him back but could manage only a guttural groan.

"What was that?" he said, startled.

"It's all I've got," I replied in my long-shoreman's voice.

"Wow, you have a problem!" he sympathized.

I went up to the conference leader, sure that he was going to tell me to go back to my room and stay there. But instead he said, "If I can hear you, and I can, they will also."

I went up to the platform, the woman who was going to set the world straight, with my Bible in one hand and a bottle of Chloraseptic in the other. Quite honestly, my message sounded like a bad frog joke.

My attitude had been wrong when I arrived, but by the time I left, it had been adjusted. The taste of humble pie lingered on my palate. It's not the kind of gift any of us looks forward to receiving, but an experience like this can be a helpful corrective to keep our sights properly focused. When we're not seeing clearly, we're bound to stumble. When humility keeps us grounded in the truth, we're ready for anything.

This day, Lord: Thank you that my identity is grounded in you, not in my own self-understanding. I want to live every aspect of my life in the humility of your truth. Amen.

Over to You, Lord

Prayer is critical to unwrapping the gifts of everyday life. The first prayer from my lips in the morning is to acknowledge God. I thank him for my life that day. At some point, I won't have the chance to wake up to a new day in this life. I don't take my time here for granted. After that I pray immediately for my family.

I had to teach myself to think of God first when I wake up. That did not come naturally to me. I'm so absorbed that my first natural thought is myself: *Oh, it's morning; I gotta get up.* Morning has always been difficult for me. If I first think of the Lord, however, I am able to move into that day with greater expectation, recognizing that it's a privilege to have the opportunity to walk through a new day with him.

For me, praying and praising first in the morning is a sacrifice. But God asks for the sacrifice of praise, which is the fruit of our lips giving praise to his name. I've found that it must please his heart, because he blesses me with a better attitude. Instead of a drudgery, morning becomes the sweet part of the day.

Throughout the day, I say a lot of "help" prayers. They sound like this: "HELP!" God is real familiar with these. Frequently, I'm asking for protection from myself. I used to think that my biggest problem was other people. Then I figured out they couldn't drag out of me anything that wasn't already there.

Because I'm short and petite, everything I do is short and petite. It gets a little repetitious at times, but it's my style. I write best in short pieces. I speak best in short pieces. On a daily basis, I also pray best in short pieces. Not that I don't have longer conversations with God, but most of the time I call out to him with requests like, "O Lord, help! I'm not handling this well" or "Help, Lord! I don't know what to do."

Practicing short prayers can help you learn to pray unceasingly throughout your day. Get on the horn with him, and don't get off. "Here it is: over to you, Lord."

This day, Lord: I don't want to live my life apart from you. Prompt me to turn to you in prayer in all my circumstances, whatever the joy or the need. Amen.

$\mathcal{B}$e joyful in hope, patient in

affliction, faithful in prayer.

—ROMANS 12:12

$\mathcal{P}$ray in the Spirit on all

occasions with all kinds of prayers

and requests. With this in mind,

be alert and always keep on

praying for all the saints.

—EPHESIANS 6:18

Life Happens While You're Making Plans

$\mathcal{I}$ used to believe that God was raising me up to be a bookstore owner. I loved matching up books and people—what writing styles they liked, what season of life they were in, which topics would benefit them. I even started a small book-room in the back of my home called God's Garden. I read everything before it went out the door.

Although I wasn't a reader as a child, I became one as an adult, out of my desperate search for answers. I started my own little book outlet, believing that one day I would open the first bookstore in our little community of Brighton, Michigan.

I was wild about anything Chuck Swindoll wrote, because his books were well organized, full of content, and they included lots of quotes which I found very appealing. I also enjoyed the work of Frances Gardner, who wrote a series of small books that had a humorous perspective, which at that time was unusual in Christian writing. I read and reread Jill Renich's *To Have and To Hold,* Hannah Whittall Smith's *The Christian Secret of a Happy Life,* Oswald Chambers' *My Utmost for His Highest,* and books by R. A. Torrey. Torrey was the grandfather of Jill Renich, who was the first teacher who ever affirmed me. I met her when a friend dragged me to a speakers' and teachers' conference because I was in such bad shape. I was smoking, taking tranquilizers, and I had a heavy addiction to caffeine. My friend thought sitting under some good teaching might improve my personality.

After our first homework assignment, Jill informed me that out of twenty-five people in the class, I was the only one who had completed the assignment according to her instructions. She said, "How was it that you could hear what I said, and no one else could?"

"It was probably because I'm the only blank slate in the room," I replied. "There's nothing for me to unlearn. I have lots of empty space to store what you say."

At the end of those half-dozen sessions she said to me, "I believe you're going to be a writer, but I don't think you're going to be a speaker."

I can understand why she said that, because I was especially short on confidence in those years and I had so many addictions to overcome. God continued to surprise all of us with the ways he drew me into the ministry. It's been said that life is what happens while you're making plans. While I was making all those plans to open a bookstore, God was making his plans. I never imagined that I would ever author books. That was a dream from my child-hood, but it had died along the way to growing up. I'd buried it underneath my failures. I was a high school dropout and a teenage runaway, married at seventeen. I was agoraphobic by the time I was twenty. I did not have any other credentials for what I do today except for the grace of God, who uses the foolish for his purposes. Les, my husband, and I say to each other daily, "Oh my goodness, how did we ever get here, except for the grace of God?"

Don't hold too tightly to your future plans, because you never know what God has in store, and his storehouses are full and rich. Enjoy what he does in your life today—his good plan for you is already unfolding.

This day, Lord: Thank you that I can leave the future in your hands and focus on serving you today. Use my time and energy according to your unfolding purposes. Amen.

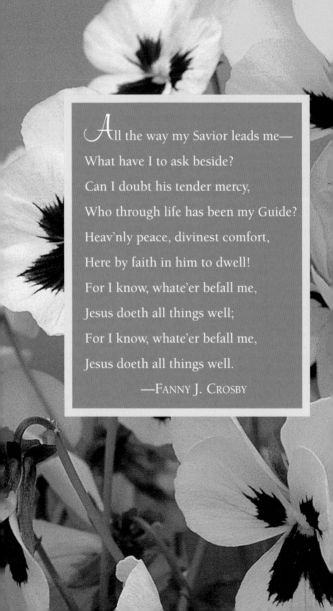

All the way my Savior leads me—
What have I to ask beside?
Can I doubt his tender mercy,
Who through life has been my Guide?
Heav'nly peace, divinest comfort,
Here by faith in him to dwell!
For I know, whate'er befall me,
Jesus doeth all things well;
For I know, whate'er befall me,
Jesus doeth all things well.

—FANNY J. CROSBY

The LORD foils the plans of the
nations;
he thwarts the purposes of the
peoples.
But the plans of the LORD stand
firm forever,
the purposes of his heart
through all generations.

—PSALM 33:10–11

Many are the plans in a man's
heart,
but it is the LORD's purpose
that prevails.

—PROVERBS 19:21

Don't Trade Today for Tomorrow

Getting ready for tomorrow gets in my way of living in the moment. I'm always getting ready for something. I'm packing, or I have to go pick up things for a trip, or I have to go buy groceries for guests who are about to arrive. I'm always preparing for tomorrow, it seems. Sometimes I realize I lost today getting ready for tomorrow! And I wasn't guaranteed tomorrow—I only get today. I think I'd better go back and grab a little more of it.

The good thing about time is that we have it; the bad thing is that we don't have enough of it. I look at other people's lives and think, *Why are their lives so much more productive than mine?* Their pie isn't any larger than mine; it's how they slice it. I go back and look at my life and ask, "What is it that I've cluttered up my life with?" Or, "Where do I have big time-wasters?" There might be something I could pass on to someone else, or something I might not even need to do at all.

I'm not always successful at it, but when I do manage to grab a little more of today, I like to carve out an interlude for something pleasurable. Perhaps taking a half hour for a cup of tea and a new magazine. I love *Victoria* magazine (please! not to be confused with *Victoria's Secret* catalog) because they combine beautiful lines from poetry with gorgeous pictures of gardens, lovely journals, tea parties, and other things appealing to my feminine interests. I carefully set aside each issue when it comes in. I don't allow myself just to grab it and leaf through it. I save it for a special time, when I just want to refresh my own soul.

Candlelit baths are another luxury I indulge in when I can get the time. I usually have to take a shower—in and out and I'm on my way, no lingering allowed. Baths are all the more enjoyable because they're a rare pleasure. You do something often enough and it becomes commonplace. I love to surprise overnight guests with a special bath done up just for them. When my friend Lana came to stay with me, I made a big bubble bath, turned on a tape recorder with some beautiful classical music, lit candles, and sent her in.

Take a little time to stop thinking about tomorrow and simply enjoy today. This day is a gift from the Lord, and it's worth celebrating.

This day, Lord: I don't want to be so preoccupied with tomorrow that I miss the gifts you have for me today. Instill in me a spirit of celebration, that I might give thanks and glory to you, the Giver. Amen.

Tomorrow—oh, 'twill never be,
If we should live a thousand years!
Our time is all today, today.

—JAMES MONTGOMERY

Surely goodness and love will
   follow me
   all the days of my life,
and I will dwell in the house of
   the LORD
   forever.

—PSALM 23:6

Better is one day in your
   courts, LORD,
   than a thousand elsewhere;
I would rather be a doorkeeper
   in the house of my God
   than dwell in the tents of the
   wicked.

—PSALM 84:10

Remember What Matters

Candlelit bubble baths, sunset bike rides, and *Victoria* magazine with a cup of hot tea in fine china are terrific simple joys, aren't they? But how do you slow down long enough from a life hurtling past at the speed of sound to make room for them in your life?

The best way I know is, Remember what matters. As we tear through our days, so much of what we think is absolutely urgent isn't really all that important, ultimately. Let's suppose you have just found out that unexpected guests are about to arrive at your house. Suddenly you're wild with anxiety, trying to straighten up the house and swab the dust kitties out of the corners and wipe the counters and get the toothpaste splatters off the bathroom mirror. This must all be done in between pulling together a lovely little spread you can lay out for them on the dining room table, of course (after you whisk away the piles of mail and the kids' homework papers).

This is a tough one for me, because I

like to have my things in order. I don't want anything in my home to reflect poorly upon me as a creative homemaker. But you and I both know that getting everything looking just right isn't half as important as being emotionally available to those people when they come in the door. It's a big step for me to be able to say, "It's all right if the place isn't perfect, because what really matters are relationships, not appearances." So let the kitties rest, order a pizza, and enjoy your guests . . . and your intact sanity.

That's a housework example, but the principle fits just about everything: So much of what flusters us just doesn't matter. It absolutely doesn't matter. Ask yourself, What is the bottom line here? Set your sights and shape your perspectives around whatever you and God come up with in answer to that question. Hold on to it tightly, and ease your grip on all the rest. You just might find yourself unwrapping a few everyday gifts you didn't know you had.

This day, Lord: I want to slow down long enough to come into your presence and focus my attention on what really matters. You are the desire of my heart, and I take joy in your gifts because you are the Giver. In Jesus' name, amen.

Cherish the Moment

Marilyn Meberg

$\mathcal{S}$imple joys are always little things for me: a good cup of tea, for instance. If you just give me a bag and a cup of hot water, that will not qualify. A simple joy is brewed, loose-leaf tea: not too much, not too little, and steeped for just the right amount of time so the tea is neither too weak nor too strong. A perfect cup of tea is not easily done, but when it's done right, it's an exquisite pleasure.

Another delight of mine is great conversation with another person in a spirit of mutual camaraderie. It's one of my very favorite things in life. The world can fall apart, and the walls come crashing down, but I would not know it if I were involved in meaningful conversation. Now, "meaningful" is one in which we track with each other. It's reciprocal. I'm not doing all the talking; she's not doing all the talking. We share an experience on levels that surprise me and delight me and encourage me—and perhaps even better yet, leave me thinking about something in a new way.

Another simple joy is food. I have just discovered the most wonderful spinach-ricotta ravioli in a little restaurant here in Palm Desert. It's terribly fattening, and I don't know what the special ingredient is, but it puts me in orbit!

Don't miss out on the joy of little things. There are probably more of them available to you than you realize. You just need to cultivate the habit of looking for them.

Then my soul will rejoice in the LORD

and delight in his salvation.

—PSALM 35:9

Freedom from "Oughts" and "Shoulds"

What usually keeps me from enjoying life in the moment is pressure—things I have to do, deadlines, duties, tasks. That's why down time is so precious to me. Living in the moment is a lot easier when I'm not thinking about how I am going to finish x, y, and z. The tyranny of the oughts and shoulds can rob you of real joy.

I truly think it's possible to strip ourselves of the oughts and the shoulds. It just takes deliberate effort. Sometimes I'll say, "Okay, Marilyn, sit down and think of everything that's hanging over your head and then prioritize it in the order in which it *really* needs to get done." There's something about having order in my head that makes the oughts and shoulds scream just a little less loudly.

The second thing I do after I've prioritized is to take the past and project it into the present. I remind myself, "It has worked in the past. Think about those

times when you were just up against the wall and somehow you made it work. Don't think about the times it didn't! Think about the times it did work and ask, *Is there any reason why that shouldn't happen again?*" I do a lot of self-talk. I call it "taking myself into my office." And I have a two-way conversation with me and myself. Sometimes we just have to slosh our way through it.

Are you held captive by your own oughts and shoulds? You might consider a two-way conversation with you and yourself. Then put the results before the Lord and ask for his wisdom and guidance in clarifying what's truly important.

This day, Lord: Help me to clear away the clutter of the oughts and shoulds in my life as I seek the priorities you want me to establish. Amen.

I am trusting Thee to guide me—
Thou alone shalt lead,
Every day and hour supplying
All my need.

—Frances Ridley Havergal

Relief from Emotional Clutter

Listing priorities to reduce the clamor of the oughts and shoulds is one thing. Clearing out emotional clutter is another. When I have that, I do a lot of taking myself to the office.

I will frequently use writing exercises as a way to explore the unrest in my soul. For example, I will write down a question: "Marilyn, you seem to be agitated, and it's not clear what the source of your agitation is. What do you think about it?" I'll drop down a line to begin my response, and I'll just start writing. In the process, things will become clear to me that had previously been under the surface, just out of reach.

Other times when I take myself into the office, I will have a dialogue with God. "Now, what do you think this is about,

God?" I'll ask him. There are certain themes in the Scriptures that he always uses in guiding me. One theme is affirmation: "I'm going to direct you." Another is assurance of his presence: "I'm never going to leave you by yourself; I am always here." Another is his faithfulness: "I will do it. I will take care of it." Those are themes repeated in the Scriptures, so when I'm asking for his wisdom and these themes emerge, I pay attention to them. If he brings Scripture passages to mind, I will quote them with my name in them: "Marilyn, this is what I'm saying to you." It's soothing—a quiet, calming reassurance.

For Scriptures that help quiet and soothe me when I need emotional relief, I love the language of the book of Isaiah, and David's intimacy with God in the Psalms. David was a whiner; he would fuss and carry on. He didn't pull any punches in venting his emotions, so reading him is a great release. In times of distress I often return to Psalm 116, where I have marked two phrases in particular: "When I was in great need, he saved me" (v. 6) and "Be at rest once more, O my soul, for the LORD has been good to you" (v. 7). I remember the times he's been good to me. I remember the times he has come through for me. He has not abandoned me to some remote island that I don't know how to get off. He's come through for me before, and he will do it again. It is his style.

This day, Lord: Emotional clutter pulls me away from you. Quiet my anxieties with reassurance of your guiding presence. Amen.

Speak, Lord, in the stillness,

While I wait on Thee;

Hushed my heart to listen

In expectancy.

—E. MAY GRIMES

The LORD is my shepherd,
I shall not be in want.
He makes me lie down in
green pastures,
he leads me beside quiet waters,
he restores my soul.
He guides me in paths of
righteousness
for his name's sake.

—PSALM 23:1–3

Accept Others as They Are

When I was a child, we lived in a succession of small rural communities in the state of Washington because Dad pastored country churches. I was a voracious reader, but I was also extremely social. Wherever we lived, there were never enough kids for me to play with. That often left me feeling lonely, so I took refuge in books. To this day I cannot bear to be without a book—I keep one in my purse, I have one in the car, I take one with me wherever I go.

In one place we lived, I remember befriending a cranky old lady who lived just up the hill from us. I talked to Mrs. Boland all the time. She didn't talk back, but still I loved to go up there and just chatter and chatter in my attempts to entertain her. She would drink tea and scowl at the wall, but when I saw the corners of her mouth move, I would think, *Well, we're making progress.* My parents never understood why I spent so much time with her—but it was clear she needed me! Her daughter, Mary Boland, was three years older than I, and she began to soften toward me because I came so often to visit her mother. In fact, Mary, unlike her mother, ultimately found me good company and even sought me out.

My visits with Mrs. Boland helped me learn the value of accepting others the way they are. I think I was able to do this because of all the affirmation I received from my parents. I always knew they loved me, even when I seemed unlovable. It is usually not difficult for me to understand that God loves me. Of course, there are times when I struggle in thinking, *How can he love me when I'm doing this?* or *How can he still love me when I'm not doing that?*

You may not be fortunate to have experienced the steady love and support of your parents, but you do have a heavenly Father who loves and accepts you no matter what. As you reflect his love by reaching out to others and accepting them just the way they are, it may help you to receive his love in your own life.

This day, Lord: Thank you that you love us no matter what. Help me to grow in the knowledge and experience of that love by accepting others just as they are. Amen.

Compassion for God's Creatures

$\mathcal{I}$ remember an occasion when I was about nine years old, during a two-year period when Dad took time off from the ministry. He had been under tremendous pressure, and he needed to get away from other people's demands for a while. He bought forty acres of remote land and dubbed them Lonely Acres. And indeed they were. It drove me a little crazy because there were no kids.

If the population was scant, however, the scenery was unparalleled. Dad built us a darling little house on the edge of a wonderfully lush stream, surrounded by trees. One of our winters there was exceedingly cold, and it snowed heavily. We were housebound, and our only heat source was a wood-burning fireplace. It was my job to go out and bring in the wood from the shed where Dad stored it.

One evening when Mom and I were home alone, I went out the door to go get wood. As soon as I stepped outside, I realized we had unexpected company. There on the corner of our front porch was a little skunk, huddled up against the cold. I did what any kid would do: I invited him in to get warm by the fire! Of course, I had no thought of the possible consequences of such an encounter. It just didn't seem right that he had to stay out in the cold when he was so close to finding shelter.

I opened the door, stepped aside, and held it open. The skunk seemed to know what I was offering. In he trotted and headed immediately for the fireplace, which was built out of lava rock from Mount Saint Helens' latest eruption. He went right to the center of the slightly raised hearth and curled up like a cat. It was so gratifying.

Mother was sitting on the couch, absorbed in reading, and hadn't noticed our guest's grand entrance. As I came in and shut the door behind me, she languidly glanced over the top of her book. Then she saw the skunk.

Mother leaped to her feet in horror, dashed into the bedroom, closing the door in no uncertain terms.

The skunk remained on the hearth in his feline posture. I don't know what the deal was, whether he was deaf or half frozen or whatever, but he just did not move.

"Mom, I'm sorry," I called to her through the closed door, "but he was *cold!*"

"Let me know when he's gone!" came the reply.

It was another thirty minutes before Stinky moved. Then he suddenly got up, turned around, and walked toward the door. I opened it for him, and he went back out from whence he had come.

"Mom, he's gone!" I announced.

After I apologized for startling Mother, I asked her what she had been doing in the bedroom while waiting for the skunk to exit.

"Well," she said, "fortunately, I had another book in there! So I just sat and read."

Despite her nervous terror, she also recognized the essential compassion in my act of bringing that little creature in out of the storm to get warm.

I never saw that skunk again, but I think of the little fellow as a sweet reminder of God's compassion for all his creatures. When we reflect that compassion, we receive again the gift of God's tenderness toward us.

This day, Lord: Thank you for the gift of your tender care. Help me to reflect your compassion for all living things. Amen.

$\mathcal{T}$he LORD is gracious and
righteous;
our God is full of
compassion.

—PSALM 116:5

Sorting Through the Wheat and the Chaff

I moved to the desert two and a half years ago in a whirl. I had been on the road for ten days prior to my move from Laguna Beach to Palm Desert, so when I got to the desert, I simply stacked boxes neatly in the garage, where they remained.

I did not truly move in until just a few months ago. In December, for the first time in two years, I didn't have a book deadline and didn't have to do any traveling. I decided to tackle the garage, which was crammed full of my boxes. I was thinking I should probably just give the stuff away since I apparently didn't need it; in fact, I could no longer even remember what was packed away!

But I began opening a few boxes just out of curiosity. It was a gorgeous sunny day, and it felt kind of relaxing to peruse my stuff. As I pulled things out, I found myself saying, "Well, for Pete's sake—look at this! My Christmas dishes—when did I buy Christmas dishes?" I also found all my Christmas decorations, which I hadn't thought of, because I hadn't been in my own home for three Christmases.

I trucked all that stuff into the house and decorated for the first time in three years. I ended up emptying all the boxes, reacquainting myself with my things and falling in love with all the stuff I had thought I could live without. I sorted out what things I knew I couldn't live without and gave the rest away.

Now my garage is clear of boxes, and my house is tidy and much enriched. I was what I call sappy-happy the entire month. Just loved it!

Chances are, you have some corner of your life that could use some sorting out—boxes in the basement, clutter in the closets, relationships that have gotten tangled, daily routines that are wearing you thin. Just take the first step toward separating the wheat from the chaff. You never know what simple pleasures it might begin to open up.

This day, Lord: I want to find and cherish the wheat in my life and blow away the chaff. Thank you that I can look forward to discovering more of your grace in my life. Amen.

Blessed is the man
   who does not walk in the counsel
      of the wicked
or stand in the way of sinners
   or sit in the seat of mockers.
But his delight is in the law of the
   LORD,
      and on his law he meditates day
      and night.
He is like a tree planted by streams
   of water,
      which yields its fruit in season
and whose leaf does not wither.
   Whatever he does prospers.
Not so the wicked!
   They are like chaff
      that the wind blows away.

—PSALM 1:1–4

Everyday Gifts

Sometimes God gives us little moments of relief when we are in the middle of painful realities that won't go away. I remember one that may sound somewhat shallow when I recount it, but it was a great comfort at the time. It was on the day my husband, Ken, who had been diagnosed with pancreatic cancer, had what is called the Whipple procedure. This is exploratory surgery in which the internal organs are literally taken out of the body so the doctors can see the pancreas. The operation showed that Ken's cancer had already spread, so they just put the organs back in and sewed him up.

When the doctor came out into the lobby and told me the news, I was deluged with conflicting feelings. *Oh no, I hadn't planned for this! What about the kids?*

Within about ten minutes, an idea suddenly sprang to mind: *Hey—I'm in*

Fullerton. Angelo and Vinci's restaurant is here. They make the best pizza in the world! I will go to Angelo's with my kids and these dear friends who sat with me through the operation.

Several days later, when Ken was able to function, I told him about this incident.

He laughed. "What a sensible thing!" he said. "And did you go get pizza?"

"Yeah, we did."

"What kind did you have?" he asked.

"You know the kind I always get—pepperoni; and they have such great sauce."

"But they have great sausage, too. Did you get sausage?"

"Well," I said, "you know, we couldn't eat everything on the menu."

As I recall this story, I think, *Isn't it silly?* Here I was in the midst of throbbing, drum-beating, awful news, thinking, *I'm in Fullerton—Angelo and Vinci's is here.* Psychologically, of course, that's what defenses do for us when we're overwhelmed. God has created within each of us the ability to find comfort. I wasn't defending against the thought that "this isn't true"; I was defending against the onslaught of how very true it was. These little God-given moments allow our emotions a needed reprieve, because the realities can be so overwhelming, we just can't carry them all at once.

In the midst of that pain, God graciously made provision of what I think is another one of life's joys—good pizza. It was a pleasure that Ken and I had enjoyed together many times. When we were first married, we'd found a place in Garden Grove that made incredible pizza, but it was torn down to make way for office buildings. We grieved until we discovered Angelo's. They had our kind of crust—not too thick, kind of thin and crisp.

Ken also asked me, as I knew he would, "What did you do when the doctor gave you the news?" I told him about the overwhelming emotions that hit me. But I also told him that, in honor of him, we got pizza. Ken smiled warmly and said, "That's really the only sensible thing you could have done under the circumstances."

This day, Lord: When painful realities seem overwhelming, help me to find relief in the everyday gifts you provide. Amen.

Loving in
the Moment

$\mathcal{W}$hen we were hit with the diagnosis
of Ken's pancreatic cancer, I realized the
here-and-now-ness of life. Talk about shift-
ing your focus to the moment—I had
absolutely no control over the future. And
in one sense, I wasn't even sure there was
going to *be* a future. I had been used to
thinking ahead with pleasure about when
Ken and I were going to go here or there
and do such-and-such. Ken was a great
planner, and some of that had rubbed off
on me. But the news brought both of us to
a screeching halt. We were very focused on
here and now because there wasn't any
promise of there and then.

God had allowed this turn of events.
He was saying, "Honey, I'm in charge not
only of life but of the number of days you
have. I'm in charge of the pain that you're
going to have with this, and I'm in charge
of the joy that comes with the pain."

Living in the moment with loved ones
means loving in the moment. Tomorrow is
not guaranteed.

I spent this past Christmas with my grandkids, Ian and Alec, who delight my heart. My favorite Ian-moment happened one day after we went to the park along with his mom and little brother and then got Happy Meals at McDonald's. All the way in the car I was acting just insane. Ian never knows what I'm going to do next, and he loves it. As we were driving back to their house, Ian said, "Mama, are we taking Maungya home?" (He named me this when he was fifteen months old.)

"Yes, Ian," his mom replied. "But it's only for a little while, because after she visits with us, she has to go back to her home."

Ian turned to me and said, with slightly lowered lids and a tilt to his head, "I *so* enjoy being with you."

Of course, I immediately melted into the floorboards. It was a moment I will never forget.

Cherish your moments with loved ones. Gather them up in gratitude for the joy they bring you today, and leave the future with the One who holds tomorrow.

This day, Lord: Keep me from rushing past my loved ones in pursuit of my own agendas. Make me sensitive to opportunities for letting them know how much I cherish their presence in my life. Amen.

Practice Gratitude When Things Go Wrong

The prayers I find myself saying most often are, "Be with me" and "Thank you, Jesus." In Flannery O'Connor's short story "Resurrection," Mrs. Turbin (who is a terrible character but does have at least one good habit) is always saying, "*Thank* you Jesus, *thank* you Jesus." There's something about the sound of that phrase that is musical and lyric. It has a nice rhythm. I say it probably a hundred times a day.

Sometimes I have to remind myself to thank God for the things that don't work, appliances included. The other day while I was making lunch, I heard a sound outside I didn't recognize. It was a very loud, pounding sound. The gardeners were out there doing their thing, and I thought maybe they were using some new tool.

I walked around the kitchen counter toward my front door. To my horror, I saw water cascading under the door in torrents, as if someone were standing outside the front door, aiming a fire hose into my house.

I soon ascertained that one of the sprinkler heads had blown off, flooding my home with water. I realized immediately that after the carpet—just a few inches away from the advancing tide—the first thing to suffer the onslaught would be my prized walnut desk, with all my important papers in it and my briefcase tucked under it, and then my bookcase with a collection of precious volumes over a hundred years old. I turned and ran down the hallway, grabbed all the towels I could find, and raced to sandbag the door and the corners of the floor-to-ceiling window, which seemed about to burst under the water pressure.

After the sprinkler was shut off and disaster averted, I kept praying, *Thank you, Jesus, that I was here when this happened. Thank you, Jesus.* I was reminded once again that "stuff doesn't work." It's easy to get complacent and forget that God holds all things together. Because he does, we don't have to.

This day, Lord: When things go wrong, help me replace frustration with thanksgiving that you hold our world together. Nothing can disrupt your loving care. Amen.

Savor the Moment

Years ago I accompanied my mother on a trip to Europe. She and my father had been all set to go, when Dad backed out at the last minute. My mother was a kindred soul; she knew I adored Europe, and she was eager for me to have this experience. She offered to take me with her and pay my way for the three-week excursion. Ken was in graduate school, immersed in papers and exams, so off I went.

I was pregnant at the time, but I didn't know it yet. I couldn't understand why I was feeling so nauseous. I didn't want to tell Mother, because I was afraid she would worry.

One night we were sitting in our hotel room in Paris, and I was feeling just cross-eyed with nausea. I was thinking what a rotten companion I must be for Mother. I was also thinking about the bus ride we had just taken. The girls across the aisle from me had been sharing a box of Ritz Crackers. I had never liked Ritz Crackers before, but on the ride I had been coveting their box lustfully. Now, back in the hotel room, I couldn't stop thinking about that box of crackers. I wanted them so badly, I thought I would die from craving them.

It turned out that we had arrived back in Paris from our bus tour on Bastille Day. This was fitting, because while I was wildly nauseous, the city was wildly drunk. After we'd gotten off the bus and walked the two blocks back to the hotel, I could not control my squeamishness anymore. I walked over to the curb and threw up. But there were others doing the same; I felt terribly Parisian.

Mother turned around to see me performing in the gutter as a number of others were and stopped dead in her tracks. "Marilyn!" she exclaimed and rushed over to my side.

I gathered myself together and said to her, "I was just savoring the moment, Mom."

Now, sitting in the hotel room at midnight on Bastille Day, I finally confessed to my mother how nauseous I'd been all along, how I hadn't wanted to be a sick traveling companion, how I'd been afraid I might ruin her trip, and how desperately I'd wanted those girls' Ritz Crackers.

"Marilyn," she said ponderingly, "I wonder if you're pregnant." At first I denied such a possibility, but she was right, and after an exam with a French doctor (that is another story) I had to fly home suddenly because I was in danger of losing the baby. But I didn't—today the baby is my six-foot, five-inch Jeff.

The next morning my mother went right out and bought me my very own box of Ritz Crackers. She spoke fluent French and negotiated a good price. As she handed the box to me, she said, "I hope you will savor these."

Indeed I did, as I savored many moments with my mother on that trip. On that same trip we were encouraged to leave John Knox's home in Scotland because something set us off and we were laughing so hard, we created a disturbance. After the dour guide began glowering at us, we went out in the street, leaned against the house, and just pealed with laughter.

For the rest of the trip Mother would turn to me and ask, "Are you feeling like savoring the moment?"

If you're having trouble slowing down long enough to enjoy life's simple gifts, my advice to you is this: *Savor the moment.* Start by taking yourself, and life, less seriously. You'll find out well enough which are the things you *do* have to take seriously—so just let the rest go! God has it under control.

This day, Lord: When I take myself or my problems too seriously, prompt me to lighten up and savor the moment. Amen.

$\mathcal{O}$ time, arrest your flight! and you, propitious hours, arrest your course! Let us savor the fleeting delights of our most beautiful days!

—ALPHONSE DE LAMARTINE

Simple Life
with God

Sheila Walsh

Catching Sight of Eternity

When I think of simple joys, the first picture that comes to my mind is my son. One of the gifts God gave me when Christian was born was a new set of eyes for things I hadn't seen in a long time.

Last fall, for example, we came back from a trip to find the patio deck knee-deep in leaves that had fallen off the big trees in our backyard. My immediate impulse was to think, *Oh no, what a job it's going to be to rake them all up.* Christian took one look and exclaimed, "Yeah!" He brought me to my senses. We put our boots on, ran out onto the deck, and had a wonderful time kicking our way through the leaves.

One of the gifts children are naturally graced with is to see some of the beauty God has given us that adults rush past every day without noticing. Perhaps this is because they so easily let go of things that aren't going to make much difference in the long run. Children celebrate the simple moments. These are the moments that have eternity written all over them, because they have to do with God. I love this quality of the eternal in children.

My life is so busy in so many other areas, I feel as if God gave me Christian to keep me sane. He is now two years old, and we pray together each night at bedtime. After I say the prayer, he names all the people he wants God to bless. I say, "in Jesus' name" and he adds, "Amen." Christian knows that whenever something really good happens, I sometimes say, "Yeah, God!" The other night after he said, "Amen" he added, "Yeah, God! You're beautiful." So are you, Christian.

This day, Lord: Help me to look past the distractions of temporal concerns and see life in light of eternity. Amen.

Gifts from the Heart

$\mathcal{A}$nother simple pleasure is extending and receiving gifts from the heart. When Barry and I returned from a concert in New York a few weeks ago to promote a new CD I'd just released, Barry knew I was really tired. He disappeared for a little while as I was rocking Christian to sleep. When I came back into our room, I saw that he had put pillar candles all the way around our bathtub and lit them. He put lovely aromatherapy bath bubbles in the water, and he brought in the CD player we keep in another room and put on some beautiful classical music, which he knows I love.

"Go in there and close the door," he told me. "And for the next hour, just relax."

It was a simple interlude when I didn't have to do or think about anything. The reason it meant a lot to me was because Barry knew just what would be soothing for me. Sometimes when people give us presents, although we may appreciate the gesture, the gift shows that they really don't know much about us. One of the things I love about Barry is the thoughtful way in which he selects gifts for me, because they reflect how well he knows me. Gifts don't mean a lot without relationship.

One of my best friends goes through a very hard time at Christmas each year because it rubs in how few people in her life really know her. How many times do we run out and get something in a hurry because we have to cross somebody off our list? Barry and I have started a tradition with Christian of praying over every single Christmas gift we buy. We want it to say more than "You're loved." We want it to say, "It's Christmastime, and we're celebrating the gift of Jesus Christ. But we're also celebrating the gift of you."

People long to be known and loved for who they are. Gift giving is one way of meeting that deep need. Take time to pay attention to other people, to notice who they are, and to help overcome their loneliness. Simple gifts from the heart are a way of saying, "I love you."

This day, Lord: Guide me to an opportunity for giving from my heart to someone who needs assurance that she is known and loved. Amen.

To see a world in a grain of
sand
And a heaven in a wild flower,
Hold infinity in the palm of your
hand
And eternity in an hour.

—WILLIAM BLAKE

$\mathcal{N}$ow that you have purified yourselves by obeying the truth so that you have sincere love for your brothers, love one another deeply, from the heart.

—1 PETER 1:22

$\mathcal{T}$his is the message you heard from the beginning: We should love one another.

—1 JOHN 3:11

Expand Your Horizons

While I was growing up, every Saturday and every Sunday after church would be the time we would go on a family walk or bike ride or enjoy some outdoor activity together. It's a joke in my family that I would always go as long as it wasn't on the sidewalk. Weekend outings had to be on grass or beach. To me, sidewalks were associated with Monday through Friday, with the school bus, with doing all the things you *had* to do. But weekends meant leaving the pavement behind and heading outdoors. Not even the rain stopped us, because we all loved rain—in Scotland, we had lots of it.

When we'd pack up for a picnic, Mom would make my favorite tomato sandwiches. Off we would go to one of several forests in that area of Scotland, or down to the beach. I have photographs of us bundled up in heavy sweaters, because it was often cold by the water's edge. But in those pictures you can see delight in our eyes.

After my dad died when I was five, my mother and brothers and I became a close-knit little team. Because we didn't have a lot of money, my mom couldn't take us many places, so she tried as best she could to bring the world to us. She would choose a different classical composer each Sunday—Grieg or Tchaikovsky or Beethoven, for instance—and then tell us a story about him before playing the music. It made my world feel very, very wide, because of the way my mother introduced it to me.

When I think of happy scenes from childhood, images come to mind of eating tomato sandwiches on a cold beach in Scotland on a Sunday afternoon or listening with rapt attention to a concerto while imagining the life of the man who composed it. What will your loved ones recall? Choose something simple to do with them—a nature walk, reading aloud from the classics, playing a selection of music—that will expand your horizons beyond immediate concerns and give you a sense of delight in life.

This day, Lord: Help me to grow in my understanding of the wonders of your world, for my benefit and to bring joy to my loved ones as well. Amen.

$\mathcal{G}$reat wide, beautiful, wonderful
world,
With the wonderful waters round you
curled,
And the wonderful grass upon your
breast,
World, you are beautifully dressed.

—MATTHEW BROWNE

$\mathcal{T}$he heavens declare the glory of
God;
the skies proclaim the work of his
hands.
Day after day they pour forth speech;
night after night they display
knowledge.

—PSALM 19:1–2

God Is Always with You

Because my mother was a widow, we never had much spare cash. But she never seemed anxious about money, so I never worried about it growing up.

I have a vivid memory of my brother Stephen, who was two years younger than I, at a stage when he was just growing and growing and growing. Every week, it seemed, he would add another inch. My mother needed long pants for him, but she didn't have the money.

One night while we were having a time of prayer, Mom prayed for long pants for Stephen to wear to school. I thought it was kind of weird, as if God kept spare long pants on hand and might simply drop them down.

A few nights later the wife of one of our church elders came to visit us. She happened to be a really good friend of my mom's. As she was leaving, she gave us a small parcel and said, "These are some things of my son's that are too small for him, and I thought you might make use of them."

Inside were two virtually brand-new pairs of long pants. My mother was deeply grateful, but she didn't seem surprised. She just led us in thanking God. I have many memories like that from my childhood. I grew up without a shadow of a doubt that God was alive, because we needed so much and he showed up so regularly.

This confidence has continued throughout my life, even at the very worst moments. Occasionally, when I have spoken about my time at a psychiatric hospital or my bouts with depression, people will ask, "Did God feel a million miles away?" And I will think, *No, absolutely not. I can't think of a moment in my life when God seemed a million miles away.* There have been moments when I didn't want to talk to him, but he always seemed very close to me. I think that's a legacy of having a godly mother who lived out her faith in front of me, day after day. I want that for Christian.

The Scriptures are filled with reassurances that God is always with us. Do you need a boost for your spirit today? Hold fast to this truth: God is always with you.

This day, Lord: I cling to the truth that you are always with me. I want this assurance to flow through me to the loved ones in my care. Amen.

Be not dismayed whate'er
betide,
God will take care of you.
Beneath his wings of love abide,
God will take care of you.
God will take care of you,
Through every day, o'er all the
way;
He will take care of you,
God will take care of you.

—Civilla D. Martin

Clearing the Clutter on Purpose

Clearing away the clutter in my life is an area I focus on quite intentionally. I have realized that one of the reasons I got into trouble earlier in life was because I lived a very cluttered life. I said yes to everything. I don't remember ever saying no to anyone. I was always thinking, *Here is a chance to do something for the Lord; therefore I should do it.* I sing and I speak and I write books, and I do a million and one things. There has been no lack of possibilities. But I have learned a valuable lesson: It's not enough simply to identify the big opportunities.

When I lost my way in life and really hit a wall, God spoke to me in a different way than he ever had before. I found a plumb line for my life: a sense of why I'm here and what God has called me to do. It has made my life so much easier, because I believe God has called me to minister to women, and I love doing that. If something comes along that sounds like a great opportunity but doesn't fit with what God is calling me to do, I say no. I know there will be somebody else God has equipped for it.

To carry out my calling, I still have to discipline my mind. Paul exhorted us to bring all thoughts captive in obedience to Christ. When I feel myself growing anxious, I'll take some time out, sit down, and consciously bring everything that comes to my mind to the Lord.

The discipline of evaluating opportunities in light of my calling has given rise to a new intentionality in how I live each day: what I say yes to, what I say no to. Sometimes the opportunities are just simple things. I used to love to go see movies with a couple of friends, but I no longer do that in this season of my life. The obvious solution might seem to be, get a baby-sitter. I might seem weird because I don't go out a lot at night. But this is a specific season of my life. Christian won't be two forever. One day he'll be twenty-two, and I'll wonder where the time went.

Barry and I consciously live a more simple life. Our favorite evening family activity with Christian is to put on our jammies and play a game. When I'm on the road, of course, the routines have to shift, because we have certain commitments we have to maintain. But even then we follow the rhythms of my ministry with our team of women.

I've learned some simple lessons about clearing the clutter from my life. If I feel anxious, I immediately take it to the Lord. If I feel angry, I immediately take it to the Lord. In earlier years, I got into trouble by letting my life pile up inside me, like a garbage disposal unit that just got more and more compacted every day. I try now to keep a very short, immediate account with the Lord so that I don't let things build up inside me. I keep short accounts with my friends, too.

Take your clutter to the Lord today. Then you won't have to drag it around with you tomorrow.

This day, Lord: I want to keep shorter accounts with you. Show me the unnecessary clutter in my life, and give me a greater clarity of purpose as I make choices based upon my priorities. Amen.

$\mathcal{T}$hen make my joy complete by being like-minded, having the same love, being one in spirit and in purpose.

—Philippians 2:2

$\mathcal{W}$hat a friend we have in
Jesus,
All our sins and griefs to bear!
What a privilege to carry
Everything to God in prayer!
O what peace we often forfeit,
O what needless pain we bear,
All because we do not carry
Everything to God in prayer.

—Joseph M. Scriven

Though we live in the world, we do not wage war as the world does. The weapons we fight with are not the weapons of the world. On the contrary, they have divine power to demolish strongholds. We demolish arguments and every pretension that sets itself up against the knowledge of God, and we take captive every thought to make it obedient to Christ.

—2 Corinthians 10:3–5

Focus on the Here and Now

Sometimes we go through experiences that shift our focus from what's up ahead to what's here and now. We are much more likely to slow down and receive the daily gifts of life when we are not mentally racing ahead.

One experience that is making us more aware of each moment is the suffering my mother-in-law is undergoing with terminal liver cancer. During Christian's first two years, Barry's parents were with us almost every weekend. It was really wonderful, because it meant that if Christian wasn't with me or with his dad, he was with his grandma and grandpa. This past Christmas, as the cancer accelerated, it dawned on us that this wouldn't be possible anymore.

There's something about the arrival of a child or the departure of a loved one that makes you focus intensely on family relationships. I recently saw the movie *Step Mom*, which I had thought was going to be a silly comedy. But it was very moving, especially in the Christmas gifts that Susan Sarandon's character, who is dying of cancer, gives to her children: a magician's cape for her son and a quilt for her daughter, embroidered with family pictures and happy memories. Barry and I have a chest in which we keep special things of Christian's, such as the jar from his first baby food. Whenever he breaks one of his little plates and cups, I keep a piece of the china. Someday I'm going to make something with all of them.

As I watch Christian changing with each day that goes by, and as I see my mother-in-law descending into illness, I am much more aware of every single day. I decided to take a camcorder with me to the next women's conference and ask each woman on our team to record a message for Eleanor. I will send her the tape so in her worst moments she has something tangible that says, "I love you, and I'm praying for you, right now."

I'm also recording Eleanor's story for Christian, for when he's older and she is no longer with him. I want her to talk about what she was like as a young girl, how she felt when she met Christian's grandpa, how they felt when they knew they were going to have a child—Christian's father, Barry, is an only child—and how they felt when they knew a grandchild was on the way.

These are things I'm doing to make sure that life doesn't just rush past me, to make sure I notice the important things. I might not have been as attentive to them if life was just rolling along without the threat of an imminent loss.

I've had some wonderful experiences during this difficult event, such as the time I was with Eleanor during one of her worst episodes. "Mom, are you afraid?" I asked her.

"No, I'm really not afraid," she replied.

Sometimes in the early years of a child's life, and the later years in the life of a Christian, God graciously draws very, very close. I've seen that a lot in Eleanor, because she has struggled over the years with her personality and temperament. But now, in what are most likely the final days of her life, when she has perhaps even more reasons to complain, I see in her a genuine peace and an assurance of God's presence.

In your concern for the future, don't look past the here and now. God has special gifts waiting for you.

This day, Lord: I don't want life to rush past me. Help me to focus on the here and now, so I can see more clearly how you are at work in our lives. Amen.

$\mathcal{T}$herefore do not worry about tomorrow, for tomorrow will worry about itself. Each day has enough trouble of its own.

—MATTHEW 6:34

Your Plans

Because I travel so much, my life is very affected by the weather and the airlines. Recently I had to go to Orange County for a crucial meeting, but I got to the airport only to find that my flight had been canceled. I went up to the counter attendant and asked if there was any other way they could get me there.

"Well, I can fly you into Los Angeles, but after that you're on your own. You could drive to your destination," she suggested.

"That's okay; if you can get me out there, I'll figure out what I'm going to do next," I told her.

Once on the plane, I found myself sitting beside a woman who was well into her third drink when she asked me what I did for a living.

"I work with five other women, and we travel around the country, speaking to women."

"What do you talk to them about?"

"We talk about hope," I replied, "and about joy, and about peace."

"I need to know you," she said.

For the next four hours she poured out her life to me. I had the opportunity to pray with her and get her name and address to send books to her. She also made plans to come to one of the Women of Faith conferences in her area. Later I thought, *I wasn't supposed to be on this flight; I was supposed to be on a flight that was much more convenient for me. But God knew which flight I was supposed to be on.*

I'm learning to say yes to God, even when I don't get it. This has not been an easy lesson, because I'm kind of a control freak. I like things the way I've planned them. But I'm finally beginning to learn that God is in control. My job is just to show up.

On the return leg of that same trip I arrived at the Orange County airport at eleven o'clock in the morning. My connection was through Dallas. *No problem,* I was thinking; *there's no snow in Dallas.*

When I got to the counter, I learned that my flight had been canceled due to fog in Dallas. "Is there no way I can get home?" I asked. "I haven't seen my son in three days."

"Well," came the reply, "you can drive down to LA and catch a flight seven hours from now."

I drove to LAX and sat for seven hours.

This time I was seated next to a businessman who asked what I was doing. After I told him, I learned that he'd been the agent for many big names in Hollywood.

"You know, it's funny," he observed. "I've worked with a lot of people who are very successful, but so few have any peace."

I began to talk to him about the goodness of God and suddenly found myself weeping. *Oh great, he's probably thinking I've lost my marbles,* I thought.

But he observed, "It's really unusual to meet anyone who feels passionately about what they do." After further conversation he made plans to bring his wife to one of our conferences, and he accepted an invitation to come as my guest even though it's a women's event.

It's okay to make plans. However, if they detour suddenly, look for God in that moment. He's probably going to be there.

This day, Lord: Forgive my impatience with interruptions. Sensitize me to how you are at work in the "detours" from my plans. Amen.

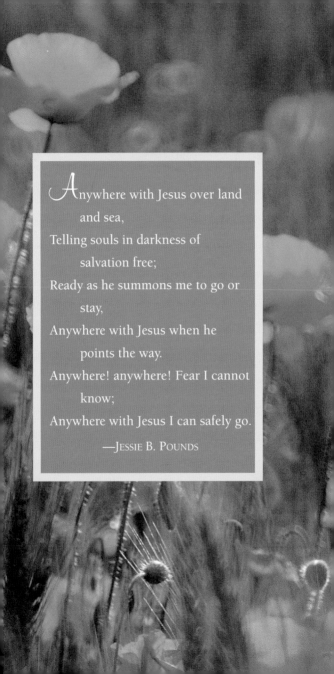

$\mathcal{A}$nywhere with Jesus over land
and sea,
Telling souls in darkness of
salvation free;
Ready as he summons me to go or
stay,
Anywhere with Jesus when he
points the way.
Anywhere! anywhere! Fear I cannot
know;
Anywhere with Jesus I can safely go.
—JESSIE B. POUNDS

$\mathcal{M}$ay he give you the desire of
your heart,
and make all your plans succeed.

—PSALM 20:4

$\mathcal{T}$he plans of the righteous are
just.

—PROVERBS 12:5

$\mathcal{Y}$ou are my portion, O LORD;
I have promised to obey your
words.

—PSALM 119:57

Jesus Is Here

$\mathcal{I}$t is hard to rest in God when life keeps us scrambling from one demand or crisis to the next. Yet those are the very times when we are most in need of depending utterly on him.

One of the passages that has helped me most in the last year is when the resurrected Christ appears to his disciples while they are hiding in fear of the Jews. He greets them with "Peace, be still!" Their fear is replaced by joy. Nothing outside those four walls had changed. There was still an angry crowd in the streets. They were still living in a terrible time. But because Christ was there, everything had changed.

Here is a truth that will sustain me no matter what life brings: *Christ is still here.* When he walks in, it doesn't mean everything outside is okay. It means I'm inside, and I'm okay, because he is here with me.

Jesus frees us from the enemies who attack us from the outside. But he also frees us from the enemies who attack us within. I have found John 8:32 to be a very liberating Scripture: "You will know the truth, and the truth will set you free." I understand this passage differently than I used to. Now I think it means bringing the whole truth about me, the good with the bad, before Christ. If I am angry or fearful or in despair, I can bring it safely to the Lord. I can accept the truth about myself, because I have been forgiven and set free.

When you stand up in front of eighteen thousand women, what you share has to be true whether you have just been diagnosed with breast cancer or your husband has just left you or you didn't get to bring your baby home from the hospital. Sometimes we hear the message from well-meaning Christian brothers and sisters, "If you just have enough faith, everything will work out." This is not helpful. It places the dependency on us. My motto is, Life is tough, but God is faithful.

When the disciples were caught in a storm on the Sea of Galilee, they cried out to Jesus in terror, "Teacher, don't you care if we drown?"

Christ stood up and quieted the waves. Then he asked them, "Why are you so afraid?" Even though the circumstances are terrifying, Christ is never afraid. And we are never alone. He is with us, and he has set us free.

This day, Lord: Thank you that in you I have been set free. Drive away my fear with the truth that you are here with me. Take my eyes off the storm and keep them focused on you. Amen.

Be still and know that I am
God; I will be exalted
among the nations, I will
be exalted in the earth.

—PSALM 46:10

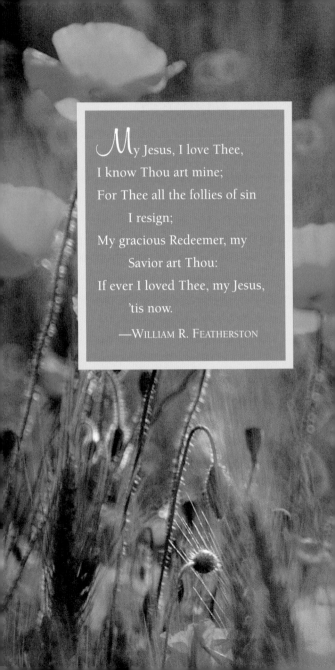

My Jesus, I love Thee,
I know Thou art mine;
For Thee all the follies of sin
 I resign;
My gracious Redeemer, my
 Savior art Thou:
If ever I loved Thee, my Jesus,
 'tis now.

—WILLIAM R. FEATHERSTON

Listen to Your Friends

A top priority in my life is maintaining long-term friendships. There's nothing like being with people who have known you for years and who love you enough to speak the truth to you. Two of my dearest companions are Nancy, who has been my best friend since we were fourteen, and Marlene, whom I used to live near in Los Angeles. I am also fortunate to have as a spiritual mentor an elder in our church, with whom I have met regularly for thirteen years. This godly man knows everything about my life. He is a source of great strength and support.

I remember one occasion on which Marlene and I were driving into LA, through traffic that was even worse than usual. Everything was going slightly wrong. I was supposed to be the host on a TV project she was doing. But she hadn't organized it very well, and it was all beginning to fall apart. I was annoyed, because my time was at a premium and I thought she should have planned it better.

When the day was over, Marlene sat down with me and said, "Sheila, I need to tell you something. You've really hurt me today."

I immediately began gathering my self-righteous defenses and proceeded to tell her how she needed to get her act together.

"It's not that anything you said wasn't right," she broke in. "I know I should have been more organized. It would have been just fine if you had told me this could have been more successful if I'd handled it differently. It's the way you said it."

She went on to tell me about some of the things that were going on in her life at the time. I felt ashamed as I listened to all the reasons she had for winging her way through the project. It wasn't the words I had used but the way I had used them. Marlene was a good enough friend to tell me. How many other people had I done this to?

The gifts with which God has entrusted us are often the source of our flaws as well. God has gifted me with words, but the Enemy can distort this gift for destructive purposes. My personality and temperament are such that words can be a great danger for me. My close friends love me enough to get my attention and say, "This is not okay." They gently mirror back to me where I need God's gracious changes in my life.

Close, trustworthy relationships are vital to our growth in Christ. They are worth guarding very carefully. Friends help us see ourselves honestly, while affirming that we are loved anyway. Treasure this great gift, and watch for it—it often arrives wrapped in everyday encounters.

This day, Lord: Thank you for dear friends in my life. Help me to listen to them and learn more about my journey with you. Amen.

This Is the
Lord's Day

Thelma Wells

This is the day the Lord has made; let us rejoice and be glad in it. Each day the Lord gives us brings with it reasons to rejoice.

When my husband says, "Baby, you need to go buy two or three suits," I take delight in his care for me. When my grandbaby strikes up a conversation with me—"Hey, Grammy: love you! 'Bye"—it brings joy to my heart. When my kids come over every Sunday and my grandkids mess up my house, leaving their little dirty socks lying around, smearing their fingerprints on my glassware, I feel pleasure. I wake up the next morning and laugh. I look at my windows—and of course my house has just been cleaned—and there are fingerprints from the little fingers that had candy all over them. I look in my bathroom mirror, and I know that somebody had to climb up on the counter and put their little sticky hands on the mirror. Joy just leaps in my spirit.

When I get a thank-you card from an employee or a nice smile from one who says, "I like my job," I receive it as a gift from the Lord. I feel his care when someone gives me a gift that is precious to her heart or when my friend Barbara Johnson calls me up and says, "Hello. Whatcha doing? Just want to see what's going on." I know he is speaking to me when a lady on our mailing list emails me a different Scripture passage each day.

Sometimes the day holds surprising gifts in store. The other day I went to film a segment for a television series I'm on with a Dallas station. This is not a Christian station. But when I arrived for the session, the producer and the executive producer both asked me to pray with them. It turns out they are Christians. We prayed for the program and for the viewers who were going to see it that day—right on the set, in front of the crew. This is highly unusual for secular television, and it brought joy to me.

Rejoice in this day the Lord has given to you. He has joy waiting for you.

This day, Lord: Open my eyes to the blessings you have in store for me. Thank you for a new chance to see you at work and to give you praise. Amen.

Overcoming Distractions

What gets in the way of my ability to live in the moment is trying to do too many things at once, forgetting that if I just pick up the first thing first and the second thing next, I'll get the things done I have to get done. Instead I tend to start feeling cluttered or panicked that I can't possibly finish it all, and I don't get *anything* done right until I slow down long enough to focus on one task at a time.

For example, I have photographs in a four-drawer chest of drawers. Do you understand I'm saying *four drawers?* Someday before I die, I'm going to take a week off and put them in the photo albums I have already purchased.

Sometimes my clutter piles up when I procrastinate on tasks I wish I didn't have to do: exercise, for instance. I'm working on not hating it. I don't hate the exercise; I just resent that I have to give time to it. Once I do it I feel good. What's hard is choosing to do that instead of something else I think I need to accomplish.

I tend to be bothered most by internal distractions. The best way I've found to overcome them is to get up early enough in the morning to get the things out of the way I don't really want to do. Then they don't take up space in my mental bank all day. I do the worst first so I can put it behind me.

The most wonderful truth behind dealing with distractions is that we don't need to organize and plan with our natural ability alone. The Holy Spirit, who gives us everything we need, can lengthen or shorten time depending on what he wants us to accomplish. If we yield ourselves to him, he will order our steps according to his purposes.

This day, Lord: Keep me from becoming overwhelmed by demands and distractions. Help me to clear away mental clutter and focus on those things that are important to you. Then give me grace to do them well. Amen.

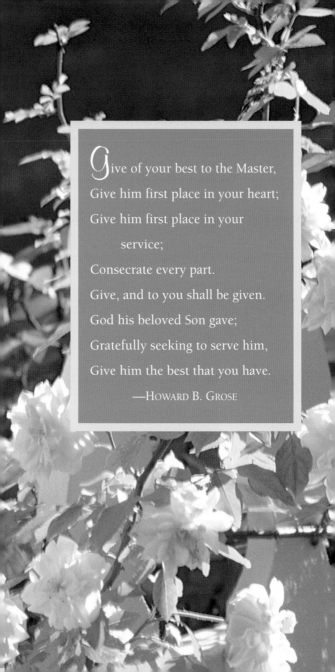

Give of your best to the Master,
Give him first place in your heart;
Give him first place in your
    service;
Consecrate every part.
Give, and to you shall be given.
God his beloved Son gave;
Gratefully seeking to serve him,
Give him the best that you have.

—HOWARD B. GROSE

Dealing with Anxiety

Nothing gets in the way of enjoying everyday gifts like anxiety. The two Scriptures I most often turn to in order to help me deal with anxiety are Jeremiah 29:11 and Philippians 4:5–6.

As you enter my house, right across from the front door you'll see a big plaque on the wall. It's parchment with gold letters that read, "I know the plans I have for you, says the LORD. Plans for your well-being, and not calamity. Plans to give you a future and a hope." When my day gets hectic and things aren't working the way they're supposed to, or when my children's lives are in turmoil, I go back to this passage: *Now, what did he say?*

In Paul's counsel to the Philippians for overcoming anxiety, he reminds them first that God is with them (v. 5). Then he instructs them to pray and ask and give thanks in all things. The God who is with them is a God of peace, and his peace will rule in their hearts and minds. Now I've had to wrestle with these truths many, many times. When I grow anxious about what is required of me, I go back to this passage. When somebody calls me with bad news, or my kids call me with problems they're facing, I go back to this passage. *What does the Word say?* Don't worry about it. Be anxious for nothing. Why shouldn't we worry about it? Because worry says to God, "Lord, I don't trust you."

But we *do* worry, and then what? With prayer and supplication, we thank God for giving us this talk again. We thank him for the process he is taking us through. Not that we want it, but because we know we're going to be the better for having gone through it. We thank him that we're not parked in there; we're not stuck. We're going *through*.

And then what does he do? He keeps his promise. He gives us peace. We don't understand it, it doesn't make sense, it's crazy, but he gives us peace we cannot comprehend—peace not only in our minds but in our hearts. That is outrageous. That is supernatural.

These are the truths I cling to when my day is disrupted by anxious thoughts. "Cast your cares upon him," Peter tells us, "for he cares for you." There is no better place to go.

This day, Lord: I cast my cares upon you, for I know that you care for me. You do not want me to be anxious about anything. Keep me in your perfect peace. Amen.

*C*ast all your anxiety on him

because he cares for you.

—1 PETER 5:7

$\mathcal{W}$hen we walk with the Lord
In the light of his Word
What a glory he sheds on our way!
While we do his good will,
He abides with us still,
And with all who will trust and obey.
Trust and obey, for there's no other
     way
To be happy in Jesus, but to trust
     and obey.

—James H. Sammis

Don't Go
It Alone

While I was growing up, I had many difficult experiences but I was always surrounded by believers. I've talked a lot about my granny (my great-grandmother), who raised me in the fear of the Lord. I remember her coming to hear me sing the lead part in an elementary school play when I was six or seven. She was an active participant in my school activities and an officer in the PTA. The first day of school she brought me in and said to the instructor, "Listen: this is a child, you are the teacher. I expect you to teach her; I expect you to discipline her; and if there's something you can't do with her, then I expect you to let me know!" Then she turned to me: "Do you understand that, Thelma?" Many a day she would come to school, even into my high school years. Her active presence in my life was a great joy to me.

My grandaddy (Granny's son) balanced out my mean grandmother. He would take me to the Majestic Theater in downtown Dallas. Because we were black, we had to sit in the buzzard roost, but still I loved to go. He also took me to parties, and he would let me ride the train through downtown Dallas. He worked on the railroad, and he would put me on the back of the train while he took his spot up front. I never knew that, however, so I'd always be wondering how in the world he could be waiting for me on the platform at the next station when I had just seen him waving good-bye to me at the last one!

My uncle and aunt, James and Allene Morris, taught me social graces. They would take me to dinner at the only fine restaurant black people could go to in Dallas, the Shalomar. They taught me how to use my napkin, where the salad fork and dinner forks go, the difference between the butter knife and the steak knife, and how to care for silver, crystal, and china. Consequently, when Allene died, she left me all her crystal and silver as well as a china cabinet to keep it in.

These godly people taught me a lot about life. They were examples to me of the love of God. I was also surrounded by believers in our church who modeled to me what God was like and taught me lessons from Scripture. Everywhere I went, there were glimpses confirming that God was real. Each summer until I was eighteen, I went to girls' camp for two weeks. I saw God in the teachers. I would drink spring-water coming from the rock. I would put my little tin cup under the springwater coming out from rocks in a stream, and it was so cold and fresh, I knew in my spirit that only God could purify the water running down a rock.

If you have days when you wonder where God is showing up in your life, think about the believers he has placed in your life to influence you in a godly way. Give him thanks for these evidences of his work in your life. Godly friends are one of God's simple gifts to us.

This day, Lord: Thank you for the believers in my life who have testified to your goodness. Show me how to bring to others the blessings I have received from these dear brothers and sisters in Christ. Amen.

I Will Fear
No Evil

$\mathcal{M}$y ability to embrace life each day
without being afraid of what might happen
is rooted in a childhood experience that
helped affirm for me the goodness of God.
When I was a child, I suffered from many
fears. I had a lot of nightmares. I was afraid
a lot of the time. This was before Daddy
Harrell died. He was blind but he noticed
the fear in me. People would come up to
me and I'd scream.

One day he said to me, "Pooch, come
here to this bed." It was a rollaway bed on
that back-alley upstairs apartment with a
screened-in front porch. "Sit down," he
said. "There's a way you can be free of your
fear, but you're gonna have to do what I tell
you. If you want to get rid of being afraid
all the time, you got to close your eyes, lay

down on this bed, and say the Lord's Prayer and the Twenty-third Psalm, over and over, one behind the other, until you don't feel scared no more."

I trusted him, so I lay down and said these prayers over and over. When I opened my eyes again, through that screen of that porch I saw the clouds up in the sky forming the bust of Jesus, and he was smiling. From that moment until this day, over fifty years, I have not been afraid again. I have traveled all over the world—including from Dallas to London during Desert Storm—and I have never been afraid.

Are you facing fears this day? Do they keep you from recognizing the goodness of God in your life? Then I would encourage you, today, to pray the Lord's Prayer and Psalm 23 over and over again until you feel the Lord lifting from you the burden of your fear. If you are busy and distracted by demands, then take this short prayer with you and pray it without ceasing: "I will fear no evil, for you are with me" (Ps. 23:4).

This day, Lord: Speak to me in the prayers I offer from your Word. Quiet my fears by the assurance of your presence. Amen.

Yes, I Believe!

Scripture is filled with encouragement for our faith because we are so vulnerable to doubt and fear when we feel overwhelmed by life. Many of us have difficulty celebrating each day as a gift from the Lord because stress is coming at us from umpteen different directions. The more confidence we have that he is active in our lives, the more we will turn toward him rather than away from him when we are stressed to the max.

We acquire this confidence gradually, across a lifetime of placing our trust in God and finding out each time that he is faithful. Over the years my prayers have changed as I continue to go through more and more adventures that show me God is at work in my life. As I look back on my early years, I recall several experiences in which the reality of God's presence in my life became very vivid. These "Yes, I believe!" encounters have stayed with me ever since, nurturing and strengthening my faith.

One of the joys of my life is remembering how Dr. Ernest Coble Estell Sr. held me up in his arms and baptized me when I was four years old. He was holding me way up high, because I was just a little thing. I had on a white baptismal robe, and all the lights in the church were off except the one over the baptistry. There was a picture behind us of John the Baptist baptizing Jesus, and a dove coming down out of heaven. I remember hearing the organist of our church playing, "Wade in the water; wade in the water . . . God's going to trouble the water." I heard Reverend Estell ask me, "Do you believe Jesus Christ is the Son of God?" And I said, "Yes." I can see this so clearly in my mind's eye: my first act of submission to God. Ever since, I have considered the ordinance of baptism so sacred that I don't think people ought to *move* when someone is being baptized.

When I was in kindergarten, I heard two dear women, Thelma Walker and Thelma Wilson, talk about how Jesus loves the little children. I heard those women talking about how Jesus wanted the little children to come to him and about all we had to do was say, "Jesus, come into my heart," and I knew that Jesus wanted me. I knew that he had come into my heart.

As an eighteen-year-old, during the Easter season I attended an extraordinary service in which an artist came to our church. Using iridescent crayons that glowed in the dark, he drew the Crucifixion. I was sitting in the balcony of the darkened church, listening intently as the artist told the story of the Crucifixion while he was drawing. When he reached the description of Jesus' blood dripping from the crown of thorns on his head and flowing from the nail prints in his hands and feet, the blood became real to me. I remember standing up and shouting in exuberance that God was our Father, Jesus was the Savior, the Holy Spirit was the Comforter.

Twice God gave me this deep assurance of his saving presence: once as a little girl, when he delivered me from all my fears, and when he confirmed to me by the power of an artist's rendition that our God reigns, that he is the Lord, that this was not a sham. Salvation was real through the blood of Jesus.

When daily living plagues you with questions about what God is up to in your life, recall how he has made himself known to you in the past. Thank him for drawing you to belief in him through these experiences. Allow them to restore your confidence in the God who never changes.

This day, Lord: Help me in my weakness and doubt. Strengthen my faith through bringing to remembrance those significant moments in my life when your Spirit prompted me to affirm, "Yes, I believe!" Amen.

$\mathcal{T}$each me knowledge and good judgement, for I believe in your commands.

—PSALM 119:66

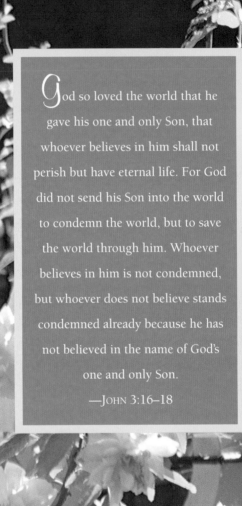

God so loved the world that he gave his one and only Son, that whoever believes in him shall not perish but have eternal life. For God did not send his Son into the world to condemn the world, but to save the world through him. Whoever believes in him is not condemned, but whoever does not believe stands condemned already because he has not believed in the name of God's one and only Son.

—JOHN 3:16–18

What Do You Really Want?

$\mathcal{A}$ few years ago I had an experience that helped me shift my focus from what's around the bend to what's here and now. I had suffered a severe burn, and while I was convalescing in bed, I decided to make a list of what I wanted out of life. I had time to think, so I got my little pad and started writing.

One goal was to make more money in order to be financially secure. Another was to spend more time with my husband, children, and grandchildren. Still another one was to be aggressively successful in my business. I wrote about ten things down, and then I went back and prioritized them. They were mostly practical things; I didn't have a lot of spiritual goals on the list.

After I wrote that down, I put it aside. The next morning was so beautiful, I went outside. I was on the back porch, and the sun was coming up through the trees. I thought about that list, and I said, "Okay, Lord, here they are. Now, Lord, tell me if I really wrote the right things down."

In my prayer he said, "You don't want these things. You want more love for me."

I took that list and threw it away. I said, "Okay, Lord, teach me. Teach me how to love you more." You know, he will do what you ask him to do.

I didn't stop thinking about these things, but I started focusing on their source instead of the things themselves. I had been on my tippy-toes, looking over into the future, thinking I was doing a great thing by clarifying what I wanted out of life. I had figured out some ways to invest more, save more, to increase my financial security.

But God just said, "Uh-uh. You can throw that away. What you *really* want is me."

Now, I have seen him do those very things I had on that paper. But they were secondary. My focus should have been on the Provider, not the provision. "I have given you power to choose what matters to you," God says to us. "And if you choose to lay up earthly treasures that moth and mildew can destroy, then you're like the fool who says, 'Wow, I got all this stuff, and I need to build me some more barns. I will eat, drink, and be merry, for tomorrow I die.'" To that the Master says, "In other words, you have not trusted me. I'm the one who gave you the ability to do well. But if you trust in me, more important than what you get is what you will be able to give. And in giving, you will get far more. You will get what you *really* want."

This day, Lord: Help me to let go of what I want out of life, and teach me to want the things that matter to you. Amen.

The only thing that counts is faith expressing itself through love.

—GALATIANS 5:6

Do not store up for yourselves treasures on earth, where moth and rust destroy, and where thieves break in and steal. But store up for yourselves treasures in heaven, where moth and rust do not destroy, and where thieves do not break in and steal. For where your treasure is, there your heart will be also.

—Matthew 6:19–21

Rejoice in This Day

Every day we must renew our minds. I don't think God means do not plan, do not look forward to days to come. I believe he means that right now is the only opportunity we have to live for him. Treat this moment, right now, as if it's your last moment, because it might be. Yesterday's blessings and progress are not today's. Be kind *today*. Lift up the Lord *today*. Share something with someone *today*.

Jesus taught us to pray, "Give us this day our daily bread." Each day we have to eat. Yesterday's meal will not tide us over. Every day has its own agenda, its own blessings, its own challenges and triumphs. Live in the moment *now*.

Each day I thank God that I can eat, drink, get dressed, seek to do his will, *now*. For those things I am tempted to take for granted, I thank God. We've got meat: that's a blessing; that's a miracle. And then I pray the most powerful prayer: "Lord, close the doors I don't need to walk through today. Open the doors that I do. Steer me away from people I don't need to deal with today. Put people in my path that I do. And Lord, don't let me waste time."

When I say don't waste time, I don't mean you can't rest in the Lord. When you're resting in him, it's not wasting time to talk to people who call you. The Holy Spirit will prompt you. You've already asked him. He says, "Okay, I'm here to comfort you, to guide you, to provide for you, to convict you. So I'm going to do that." It's not fearful; it's liberating. Not wasting time doesn't mean packing more things in. It means using our time wisely. It could be sitting down and talking to somebody for an hour or two. You might have spent time you thought you didn't have doing that, but when you come back to whatever you were doing, the Lord will give you the knowledge to get everything done or the wisdom to know you didn't have to do it today.

Of course, there's not a week that passes that I don't need the Lord's admonition to be anxious for nothing. But he will work everything out. He has ordered this day. Let us rejoice in it as a gift from him.

This day, Lord: I accept this day as a gift from you. I want to spend my time according to your wisdom and guidance. Make me sensitive to how you desire to order my day. Amen.

This is the day the LORD has
made; let us rejoice and
be glad in it.

—PSALM 118:24

Fresh Start
Joy

Barbara Johnson

*E*ach day that we live is a gift from God. Maybe that's why *today* is called "the present"! To unwrap this gift of everyday life, learn to make *gratitude* your *attitude*. When you start focusing on all the blessings God has infused into your life instead of the problems you encounter, you'll soon realize, as I have, that you're too blessed to be stressed!

All of us have plenty of opportunities to worry, but we must remember that worry never accomplishes anything—except to make us miserable. Instead of fretting about what might happen, we need to realize that God puts a veil across our way so we don't know what's ahead of us. He hides the future so that we learn to trust him for our daily existence just as simply as "the lilies of the field" do. Jesus told us the lilies don't worry about tomorrow—and neither should we.

How thankful I am for that assurance! If I had known at age twenty what lay ahead for me during the next thirty years, I would have started looking right then and there for someplace where mothers could go to resign! In God's economy, we're granted enough grace to live one day at a time, and when we spend a part of that day worrying, we're wasting the precious gift of life we've been given.

Do you struggle with worry? If you're trying to pull aside the veil to see how everything is going to turn out, try waking up tomorrow with a grateful heart that's thankful for another day to serve God and his kingdom. Get up in the morning, put your feet on the floor, and say, "Lord, thank you for this day. Thank you for another opportunity to represent you to everyone I meet in everything I do. And thank you for grace enough to handle whatever difficulties come my way." That attitude is fresh-start joy.

Windshield-wipe the past from your mind. Remember that yesterday is a canceled check, and tomorrow is a promissory note, but today is *cash*. Spend it wisely!

This day, Lord: Help me to windshield-wipe the past from my mind so I can demonstrate your fresh-start joy to everyone I meet. Amen.

$\mathcal{T}$here are two days in the
week about which and upon
which I never worry. Two carefree
days, kept sacredly free from fear
and apprehension. One of these
days is Yesterday. . . . And the
other day I do not worry
about is Tomorrow.

—ROBERT JONES BURDETTE

$\mathcal{S}$ing to the LORD, you saints of
     his;
   praise his holy name.
For his anger lasts only a moment,
   but his favor lasts a lifetime;
weeping may remain for a night,
   but rejoicing comes in the
     morning.
          —PSALM 30:4–5

$\mathcal{H}$e put a new song in my
     mouth,
   a hymn of praise to our God.
          —PSALM 40:3

Splashes of Joy

Splashes of joy are all around us—but we have to look for them with joyful eyes. For example, at the post office, I see more than just rows of mailboxes and a long line of people with saggy faces waiting for their turn at the counter. On my way in, I look at the cement sidewalk and see millions of little sparkles. When the sun hits the cement just the right way, the sidewalk shines with a million transient diamonds. They're beautiful and shiny, and they make me think of all the blessings God has given me, all the places in my life he wants me to find his blessings, and all the people he has brought into my life.

When my husband goes to the post office, he doesn't see little diamonds. He's a wonderful guy, but he doesn't go

through life bursting with joy. When he goes
to the post office, he's too busy looking for a
parking space to notice the diamonds
sparkling on the sidewalk. He has to work at
finding splashes of joy, but it's no problem for
me. So I do it for both of us.

The smallest things bring me bountiful
joy, even brief messages left on my answering
machine. A woman who writes to us regularly
and supports our ministry called and left this
quip on my machine: "Barb, may the joy-bells
of heaven ding-dong in your heart today!"
Then she hung up. That was a simple little
blessing, but it was a gift that splashed joy on
an otherwise ordinary day.

*This day, Lord: Help me to splash joy
across someone else's day. Amen.*

May my meditation be pleasing to him,

as I rejoice in the LORD.

—PSALM 104:34

The Fun of Childhood Pleasures

When I was a child, we lived in Michigan, where we had a lot of snow. On the coldest winter day, my dad used to call the fire department and have them come and flood the field next to our house so that we had our own private skating rink. We thought that was the most fun any child could possibly have! We did a lot of fun things during the winter—making angels in the snow, building snowmen, flinging snowballs. I miss that now that I live in southern California.

When I was twelve, my dad dropped dead quite suddenly one day on the way home from his preacher's duties. He had never been sick a day in his life, so we weren't at all prepared for his death. Our family went through some very rough experiences. But one thing that helped was knowing he was a Christian and that he was with the Lord. He was my first "deposit" in heaven. That's when I started looking forward to heaven while my feet were still planted on earth.

Another thing that helped my sister and me cope with the grief of losing our dad was the wonderful memories he had given us—memories like the ones we had of playing on that vacant lot he had managed to transform into a winter wonderland.

Since then other loved ones, including two sons, have become my deposits in heaven, too. When I think of my boys, it's hard not to be sad. But then I remember some of the silly things we did together and all the laughter and joy we shared during their growing-up years, and those wonderful memories push aside the grief.

These comforting memories have become cherished treasures that warm me when death's icy sadness threatens to close in on me. And they've reminded me that even in the midst of hard times, there's always a way to have fun. Sometimes you just have to look for it in unusual places. Whenever you find joy, share it—and create a memory that can light a spark on a dark day in the future.

This day, Lord: Help me to take a childlike pleasure in the good things that are all around me—and to share that joy with someone else. Amen.

$\mathcal{T}$each us delight in simple things,
and mirth that hath no bitter springs.

—Rudyard Kipling

From the lips of children and
   infants
   you, O LORD, have ordained
   praise.
      —PSALM 8:2

How great is the love the Father
has lavished on us, that we should
   be called children of God!
      —1 JOHN 3:1

Getting Rid of Excess

The clutter in my life I have to work hardest to clear away is the heaviness of carrying the burdens of hurting people. Because I spend a lot of time on the phone in our ministry, listening and encouraging heartbroken parents, I hear a lot of sad stories. My phone rings all day, so it's easy to feel dragged down by all the pain people share with me. For instance, just recently I learned of two suicides—one unsuccessful attempt and one carried through—on the same day.

As I hang up the phone from one sad story after another, I pray, "Lord, bless that person. Put your comfort blanket of love around her." Then I move on to the next letter or the next story. To keep going, I have to windshield-wipe these tragedies from the front of my vision and cling to Paul's advice to think on those things that are good and pure and lovely.

What's the best way to clear out the emotional clutter you're dragging around? The best way is to dwell on the praiseworthiness of God instead of the heartbreak of your problems. Jesus came to give us a spirit of praise instead of a spirit of despair. He, more than any of us, knows how hard life is.

Whatever is going on in your life right now, allow God to wrap around you a garment of praise and a comfort blanket of love. Praise him for who he is. Maybe you can't praise him for what is happening to you right now, but you can praise him for what he is going to do, even if you don't see evidence of what he is up to at this particular moment. Try on his new clothes. Be warmed by his comfort blanket. And clean the clutter of your old burdens out of your life.

This day, Lord: Lift my heavy burdens off my shoulders and wrap me in your garment of praise and your blanket of love. Amen.

$\mathcal{W}$hen peace, like a river,
attendeth my way,
When sorrows like sea billows
roll—
Whatever my lot, Thou has
taught me to say,
It is well, it is well with my
soul.

—Horatio G. Spafford

Choose Your Pictures

Sometimes God gives us "frozen pictures" of happy times to replace dark thoughts or unhappy memories of loved ones we have lost to death or to alienation. Dwelling on troubling images only makes the heartache worse, and it can take your eyes off the Lord. Learning to focus in a positive way on the good things you have shared in the past with this loved one will help you get your eyes back on the blessings instead of the burdens.

After our beautiful twenty-three-year-old son Tim was killed up in the Yukon by a drunk driver when his little Volkswagen was hit by a three-ton truck, his body was sent back to California in pieces, with wire wrapped around the wooden crates. I don't like to think of him that way. Instead I like to dwell on a frozen picture of him and his brothers during a happy time—the day I came home and found all four boys throwing Jell-O on the white wall in the kitchen. They were firing it out of their spoons like David slinging stones at Goliath. When I saw Jell-O and banana mush sliding down the white bricks, I didn't get upset. I just sat down with them, grabbed a spoon, and fired away. We finished throwing the whole bowl of Jell-O–banana salad against the walls *together*. Why not? After all, the mess was already made, and the boys would have to clean it up anyway.

That's one of the pictures I bring to mind when I think of my son: he's laughing with his head thrown back, surrounded by his brothers and his mom, and red Jell-O is flying across the kitchen.

Whenever you think of loved ones you have lost, choose a happy memory and freeze that picture. Then each time you think of or pray for them, instead of a fearful or heartbreaking image you will have a happy, bubbly, shining picture to fill your mind with joy and hope.

This day, Lord: I want to choose a lovely picture for that place in my heart where I am aching over a loved one. Let this be what I see when I pray for or remember this one whom you love, too. Amen.

O Joy that seekest me through pain,
I cannot close my heart to Thee;
I trace the rainbow through the rain,
And feel the promise is not vain
That morn shall tearless be.

—GEORGE MATHESON

A Change of Perspective

$\mathcal{W}$hen you can't see around the bend and the view right in front of you is enough to make you give up and sit down in the middle of the road, remember that God is in charge of what's coming. God promises us, "There is hope for your future" and "Your children will return to their own land."

When I went through the eleven-year period when our son disappeared, disowned us, and changed his name, I was in a hope-deferred situation. I learned a lot of things during that time. I learned to say, "Whatever, Lord." Whatever comes into my life comes through God's filter. Nothing will happen to me that he doesn't know about. God's not gonna say, "Oops! I shouldn't have done that to her!"

When you're stuck in a hope-deferred situation, remember that you're not at a dead end. You're just biding time in God's waiting room. It seems like we're all waiting for something. Some people are waiting for the lottery to turn up their numbers. Some people are waiting to have surgery. Others are waiting to have a baby.

(I read somewhere that the only time a woman wants to be a year older is when she is pregnant!) Whatever our circumstances, we're all waiting for *something* to happen. All of us have to cope with hope-deferred situations.

If that's where you find yourself right now, start saying, "Whatever, Lord!" instead of "Why me?" Whatever happens will come through his filter. When you're in God's waiting room, you can take heart, knowing the Great Physician is in.

This day, Lord: Instead of "Why me?" I want to say, "Whatever, Lord!" By the power of your indwelling Spirit I ask that not my will but yours be done. Amen.

Do What Jesus Would Do

Whenever you find yourself facing difficult decisions, remember that the answer to most questions is another question: "What would Jesus do?" This phrase has become real popular these days—for a good reason. It's just the right response to whatever circumstances you find yourself in.

When you're struggling with problems, ask yourself what Jesus would do. By his examples recorded in Scripture, we know he would reach out to the hurting, to the unloved, to those who are caught in sin. He would reach out with his love, and that's what we have to do, too.

As I work with hurting parents, I encourage them to love their wayward children with unconditional love. I don't mean sloppy agape, the just-do-your-own-thing kind of love, but the kind that says, "I'm going to love you and pray for you until they put a lily in my hand and close the casket over my head."

The Bible refers to secret things that will happen in our lives that we're not going to understand. These secret things belong to the Lord. Instead of being consumed by the search for answers, we just have to say, "This is one of God's secret things."

I don't know why God took my two sons; I don't know why my third son disappeared for eleven years after I found out about his homosexuality. Those things are in God's hands, and I relinquish them to him, knowing I will probably never have the answer until I get to heaven.

We all carry around the scars of "secret things" that are painful to bear. Our tendency is to ask, "Why?" Instead we could be asking, "Who?" Who else is struggling for answers to these painful things and needs our comfort?

This day, Lord: I turn over my why questions to your mysterious but loving purposes. Open my eyes to those around me who are hurting as well. Help me reach out to them the way Jesus would do. Amen.

Help me the slow of heart to move
By some clear, winning word of love;
Teach me the wayward feet to stay,
And guide them in the homeward way.

—Washington Gladden

*J*esus said, " A new command I give you: Love one another. As I have loved you, so you must love one another."

—JOHN 13:34

*P*raise be to the God and Father of our Lord Jesus Christ, the Father of compassion and the God of all comfort, who comforts us in all our troubles, so that we can comfort those in any trouble with the comfort we ourselves have received from God.

—2 CORINTHIANS 1:3–4

Be a Refresher

There are two things I'd like my kids to remember about me: that I laughed a lot, and that I was refreshing. I want to be like Onesiphorus, a man mentioned only once in the Bible. Paul said this man's visits to him while he was in prison revived him like a breath of fresh air. Have you ever heard anyone preach on Onesiphorus? Probably not. He's pretty obscure to us. But he wasn't obscure to Paul. What a joy, what an honor, to be called "one who refreshes." And what a Christlike thing it is to be an encourager. The word *encourage* means "to fill the heart," and that's what my job is: to fill the hearts of a lot of lonely, hurting, wounded people. You can imagine how pleased I was when quipster Ashley Brilliant dedicated a recent book to me, calling me "the queen of encouragement." It was the biggest joy to open up his book and read his note to me.

Through my own experience, I've learned that the best antidote to discouragement is to find someone else who is in need and share with her my energy, love, time, and attention. Try it and you'll see! As you water another, your own spirit will be lifted. I think it was the psychiatrist Karl Menninger who declared that the way to get over depression is to help another, but as Christians we know this is true because the Bible tells us to do it. This is the principle of boomerang joy: throw out your joy and it comes back to you in a way that encourages and refreshes you.

So whenever you're in need of encouragement, instead of waiting for someone to come along and lift your spirit, try being a refresher. Bring a little fresh air into another person's life, and you just might find that the invigorating breeze blows back your way.

This day, Lord: Let me follow the example of Onesiphorus. Lead me to the person you want me to encourage, the one whose heart needs filling by a loving word or an act of kindness. Amen.

A little word in kindness spoken,

A motion or a tear,

Has often healed a heart that's broken,

And made a friend sincere.

Friendship Gifts

My friend Lynda is such a joy and an encouragement to me. Being with her is like charging my batteries. One day she accompanied me to a speaking engagement somewhere. I was tired; I'd been speaking to churches and women's groups all week and was nearly exhausted. As we drove along, I sighed and said, "I'm just so *sick* of spreading my joy. I wish I could just forget it!" Just then we looked up and saw a road-side billboard, about twenty feet high, that said, "Spread your joy!"

Lynda said, "See, Barb, that's God telling you to spread your joy!" We laughed all the way to the church. And after I'd spoken to the women gathered there, one woman told Lynda my words had lifted her out of heartbreaking despair. How thankful I was that Lynda's wit had energized and encouraged me to go on.

There are still days when I feel like I just can't do it again. Inevitably on those days Lynda will call, as she did recently, and announce, "Barb, I have a message for you: Good morning, this is God. I will be handling all of your problems today. I will not need your help, so have a good day."

Lynda is always on the lookout for clippings that will work for my newsletter, or for little jokes I can put in my next book. Or she will call up my answering machine and impersonate a celebrity, leaving me a silly message from Barbara Streisand or some other star. When you've got a friend like that, you've got a treasure-house of simple gifts!

Don't take your friends for granted! Thank them for the gifts they bring into your life. And look for ways to give simple gifts back to them. Before you know it, you'll be energized by the joy you share.

This day, Lord: Thank you for my dear friends. Show me how to encourage one of them with a simple gift that will express my care. Amen.

The better part of one's life consists of his friendships.

—ABRAHAM LINCOLN

A friend loves at all times,
and a brother is born for
adversity.

—PROVERBS 17:17

*P*erfume and incense bring
joy to the heart,
and the pleasantness of
one's friend springs from
his earnest counsel.

—PROVERBS 27:9

Little Things Make a Big Difference

Sometimes the simplest things in life can make the biggest difference. Taking a nap when you need it can make the whole world look brighter and friendlier. Going for a walk with a friend on a sunny day can make your troubles seem less troublesome. Enjoying an outing with a child can put fun back into your life.

At home I have lots of ways to make a big difference with little things. For example, I like to put some ground cinnamon in a pan with a little moisture—water or butter—in my oven and turn it on very low. My whole house smells like apple pie even though it's been years since I've actually baked one. (My husband, Bill, says, "Barb cooks for fun, but for food we go out.") It's true. I don't like to cook much anymore. I've done it for decades, and I'm tired of it! But I do like to make the house smell good. I love the way turkey smells when it's cooking (even though I don't like to eat it very much). I sometimes put a turkey breast in my crock pot, and soon the house is filled with the wonderful aroma of…Thanksgiving!

The fragrance of baking bread is one of my favorites, too; for that I have to go to someone else's home, because I don't bake bread. Cinnamon is my specialty.

Pleasant scents have been proven to help relieve all sorts of ailments, ranging from anxiety and panic attacks to back pain. They seem to boost our moods no matter what the pain happens to be! Someone gave me a rose with little petals that you peel off and put in the vacuum cleaner bag. Now when I'm cleaning, the whole house smells like roses. I love that! Another trick is to dab vanilla oil on light bulbs. Pretty soon after the light is turned on, the wonderful aroma of warm vanilla fills the room.

Most of us feel a little rush of pleasure when somebody walks in the door of our house and exclaims, "Umm, something smells good!" It doesn't take much effort to dress up our homes with wonderful scents, and these little things don't cost much money. But they can make a big difference.

This day, Lord: I want to be creative in enhancing the atmosphere of my home. Thank you for simple things that can brighten the spirit and warm the hearts of those who enter it. Amen.

$\mathcal{T}$wo are better than one,

because they have a good

return for their work:

If one falls down,

his friend can help him up.

—ECCLESIASTES 4:9–10

$\mathcal{E}$ncourage one another and

build each other up.

—1 THESSALONIANS 5:11

Everyday
Thankfulness

 Every day I thank God for good health
and good eyesight and an abundance of
energy. The joy I have is a gift, too. God
infused me with it many years ago, and
I've had it every day since then. That
little bubble of joy that comes up from
inside me; it's always there, and I just
praise the Lord for it.

   Because I have this joy and energy,
I'm able to get up every morning and
happily compose a newsletter or write
books or communicate with people. God
equips us for what we need to do. I have
a tremendous amount of joy energy for
the work he has given me. Many people
say to me, "I just don't know how you
do it!" And the truth is, I don't do this
work on my own. God propels me
through each new assignment.

Every day I thank God for the gift of laughter and the ability to find funny things in the midst of tragic situations. You see, one laugh equals three spoons of oat bran, and one hearty chuckle burns up six calories. So I praise the Lord that he's given me a funny bone. Without a sense of humor, I'd be a lot heavier, not to mention sadder!

Practice thankfulness every day. Look for the humor in every difficult circumstance. (If you don't see it right away, that usually means it's sneaking up on you.)

This day, Lord: I pause and thank you for all the gifts I have right in front of me. Restore my energy and perspective with a good laugh today. Amen.

Let the peace of Christ rule in your hearts...

And be thankful.

—COLOSSIANS 3:15

Give Guilt the Heave-Ho

$\mathcal{M}$any parents feel tremendous guilt about everything that goes wrong in their kids' lives. They are unnecessarily bowed down with the weight of it. When I recognize guilt as their problem, I tell parents, "Look at the mess God had with Adam, and God was perfect! So who are you to think you can do better than God?" Then I tell them to memorize Psalm 32:1 (LB): "What happiness for those whose guilt has been forgiven!" How happy we can be! We don't have to whip ourselves with remembered sin, because we can claim that verse and stand clean before the Lord.

If you're a parent of an adult child who has strayed, remember: If there's no control, there's no responsibility. You don't have to feel guilty about what you're not responsible for. You can live a guilt-free life because God has cleared your record. The guilt in your past has been removed—it's vanished! Gone! Erma Bombeck described guilt as the gift that keeps on giving. If you keep on accepting that "gift," you're going to be unhappy, and that's not what God wants for your life.

All the parents I know did the best they could; they're not responsible for their kids' choices. All they can do now is to put those kids in God's hands and know that God loves them. He doesn't abandon parents or their children because of bad choices. In Ezekiel 34:12, God said he will go out and rescue his sheep from all the places they were scattered on a dark and gloomy day. How comforting it is for parents to know that God will go after the prodigals.

Are you carrying around a weight of guilt over the choices your kids have made? Give it the heave-ho! You'll be surprised at how much new energy you have for praising God when you're not laid low by the guilt you've been piling on yourself. Put that new energy into prayer for your loved ones and into reaching out to others who are suffering the same hurts. Then your focus will shift from "What have I done?" to "What is God doing?"

This day, Lord: Thank you for your forgiveness and mercy. I want to lay down my burden of guilt at your altar. Take my focus off my doubts and weaknesses and redirect it to your transforming grace. Amen.

Just Passing Through

$\mathcal{I}$'d like to give you one simple piece of advice for making it through tough times: Remember that we're only pilgrims; we're not settlers. One of these days, he's gonna toot, and we're gonna scoot—right out of here. Whatever you're going through right now, it's only temporary. It's not going to last forever. Soon our final exit here will be our grandest entrance there.

The promise of heaven is beautiful to me because I have deposits there. If you can get your focus squarely on the truth that this life is just temporary, you're gonna ease your grip on your home, your kids, your job, and every other earthly thing, because you'll know that one of these days you'll be out of here, and you won't be taking anything with you.

This old world is wobbling on its last legs. When a recent issue of *Time* magazine profiled some faithful people who are waiting for the trumpet to blow, I thought, *Man, isn't that true? The trumpet's gonna blow, and we're gonna go!*

One of the happiest times I've had recently was down in Carthage, Missouri, with my friend Sam Butcher, creator of

Precious Moments. In that encouraging place God revealed himself to me in a very special way. The Precious Moments Chapel and Fountain of Angels portray the most glorious perspective on heaven. I spent the three most refreshing days of my life there, just thinking about heaven and the treasures and loved ones awaiting me there.

Do you need fresh joy today? Take a little time apart to dwell on your treasures in heaven. And then rejoice, remembering that you're just a pilgrim here, passing through en route to glory!

This day, Lord: Fill my heart with the hope of heaven. Thank you for the eternal glory we can look forward to with you. Amen.

O God, give us serenity to accept what cannot be changed, courage to change what should be changed, and wisdom to distinguish the one from the other.

—REINHOLD NIEBUHR

 $\mathcal{W}$ hile we walk the pilgrim

pathway

Clouds will overspread the sky;

But when traveling days are over

Not a shadow, not a sigh.

When we all get to heaven,

What a day of rejoicing that will be!

When we all see glory,

We'll sing and shout the victory.

—ELIZA E. HEWITT

Live
Now

Luci Swindoll

$\mathcal{L}$ife's simple gifts are easily found and easily enjoyed. They don't take a lot of money, and they needn't take a lot of time. They come wrapped in simple ways of interacting with life, with the moment, with a person.

For me, simple pleasures arrive as an afternoon in which I have time to read something I really enjoy, or a chance to paint, or to ride my bike, or work in my flower bed, or take a long bubble bath, or entertain a few friends. They always spring from circumstances right at hand; I don't have to go out and buy things to make them happen. I just find a resting place in something already nearby. A simple pleasure is a place of comfort and ease, not necessarily in solitude—although I love solitude—but something that gives me pleasure in an ordinary way. It's very hard to come by in a busy life, and so it's a gift to treasure.

Stimulating Mind and Heart

One of the simplest pleasures I really love, which I just have to hit upon—it's not something I can plan—is a really rich conversation. It can happen with anyone whose mind I respect, whose opinions I enjoy, who has a sense of humor, who is free to say and be whoever and however she wants to be and I want to be. For me, that's a delightful way to pass an hour. I've had many of these times with my friends on the Women of Faith team, and they are particularly true of my friendships with Marilyn Meberg and Mary Graham. These are times of mutual bonding.

Another stimulating activity that gives me pleasure is journaling. I've journaled for twelve years, almost every day. I write about everything. Sometimes I'll choose a notebook for the year, a bona fide "journal" with dates in it; other times I'll use a book with blank pages on which I write, draw, paint, argue with the newspaper, pour out my heart, cry, praise, or just talk about my day.

I sometimes review my journals to see if I can spot trends in what I've done in the past, what I want to do now, where I'm going. They mirror myself back to me, just the way you can get a clearer picture of what's going on inside when you hear yourself pouring out your heart to a friend. You just didn't know you had it in you!

Processing life through rich conversation and personal writing can go a long way in stimulating mind and heart. Most of us have easy access to such pleasures. Don't overlook them—you might be surprised what a difference they make.

This day, Lord: Lead me into a conversation in words or on paper that stimulates my mind and heart. By your Spirit, speak to me in a fresh way about your work in my life. Amen.

Writing, when properly managed,

is but a different name for conversation.

—Laurence Sterne

As iron sharpens iron,

so one...sharpens another.

—PROVERBS 27:17

Love the Lord your God with all

your heart and with all your soul

and with all your mind.

—MATTHEW 22:37

Let your conversation be always

full of grace, seasoned with salt, so

that you may know how to answer

everyone.

—COLOSSIANS 4:6

The Simple Pleasure of Creativity

One of my favorite things in life to do is to make something by hand. I learned that very early in life from my mother, and it has stayed with me all my life. When I was a child, we didn't have a lot of money, but my mother was very creative. My father was often busy working, but he never squelched any of Mother's creative juices. She encouraged us to make things with our hands. My aunt was very artistic. We would make kites for picnics or church outings. I think humankind's greatest invention is the alphabet, and probably the second greatest is scissors. If I can use both of those, I can be content literally for hours and hours.

Andrea Grossman, a very good friend of mine who is the head of Grossman Paper Company, got me started on stickers. I love using all kinds of stickers in my journaling for my own pleasure. When I went to Africa, I used wild animal stickers to enhance my recollections. I've used this practice for years. It's just another opportunity to be creative.

One creative endeavor I have enjoyed recently was with my camera. I love photography. In the desert, the hot air balloons go up early in the morning or late in the evening. It makes for great photo opportunities. I got up early one morning, got on my bike—camera in hand—and trailed a balloon for several blocks. (I did not pedal and shoot simultaneously.) It was fun to track it all the way to a nearby field, stopping only to take pictures.

Creativity is not highly valued in our culture, but it ought to be. It's embedded in our spiritual genes. As Christians, we can delight in reflecting this attribute of the character of God. Look for a way to do something fun with your hands today. It's not an indulgence in something unnecessary. It's an expression of who you are in Christ.

This day, Lord: Draw me into deeper wonder and praise as I take pleasure in creativity, reflecting the truth that I am made in your image. Amen.

Creativity is a God-given ability

to take something ordinary and make

it into something special.

—EMILIE BARNES

*I*n the beginning God created
the heavens and the earth. . . .
God saw all that he had made,
and it was very good.

—Genesis 1:1, 31

*T*he heavens are yours, O Lord,
and yours also the earth;
you founded the world and all
that is in it.

—Psalm 89:11

*I*n the beginning you, Lord, laid
the foundations of the earth,
and the heavens are the work of
your hands.

—Psalm 102:25

Special Gifts

$\mathcal{M}$usic has such power to move the heart. I grew up with it as far back as I can remember. My mother taught it to me; she was a piano teacher for over thirty years. My grandmother played as well, and I remember hearing her play and making up tunes as she went along. She could play in any key.

My family was very musical. I played guitar; my older brother played clarinet; another brother played piano. We would often sit around the piano at night, singing in harmony. Everybody took a different part. The whole family did this, except for my father, who often worked the night shift as superintendent of a machine shop. He wasn't much of a singer, but he loved hearing us sing. He thought we were the undiscovered Von Trapp family.

At night, after eating dinner and doing the dishes, we would often listen to the radio, since we didn't have a television. But generally we would sing, simply for our own amusement—church songs, camp songs, hymns, patriotic songs, popular tunes. I can remember two or three times going to bed at about 9:45 or 10:00, when the phone rang with one of the neighbors asking us if we could go back to the piano and sing some more.

I learned later that they would all go to our window when we started, on either side of us, but usually on the side where they could best hear the music. I used to think every family sang together; I didn't realize until years later how special that experience was.

I don't play now, although I sang for fifteen years with the Dallas Opera. Now I listen mostly. I love classical music, which I was introduced to through my training. I do get to sing occasionally and enjoy that very much. When our team had a prayer time recently with Joni Tada, just before she prayed she started singing a hymn. Everybody joined in. There were about fifteen women there, and the room was filled with four-part harmony. Especially because of the significance of music in my life, this was a special gift.

God loves us in very personal ways. For me, music is a way of receiving his personal care and sharing this gift with others. What special gifts mark your own history with God? Pay attention to them. They will fill you with a sense of God's love and give you a way to share that love with others.

This day, Lord: Help me to bring joy to others through sharing with them one of the simple gifts I enjoy from you. Amen.

Find a Resting Place

During tough seasons in my life, I find it especially hard to carve out time for myself. After forty years in the corporate world and planning for retirement, I thought I'd be slowing down at this season in my life. Instead I'm busier than I've ever been.

I love the purpose of my life now: traveling with a team of women to encourage our sisters in Christ all around the country. I love knowing the women on our team and the women who keep pouring into the arenas where we speak. I know this is God's plan for me; I know he designed it all along. Although I would have had a lot more energy for this twenty years ago, in the last two decades I've learned things I couldn't have gotten any other way. I do have something to say, and it is very meaningful for other people. I have more to say now than I would have had years earlier, because I have lived through many more experiences, making mistakes and putting two and two together. I now have a chance to make use of everything the Lord has taught me—not just for me but to help others. And that's a great privilege.

Because this is such a demanding season of my life, however, I know it is very important to create time for myself—to give myself "perks" along the way. Sometimes they're as simple as reading on the plane instead of talking or working. Other times it means taking time alone at the hotel to catch my breath and regroup. When it just feels like too much, I remind myself that the Lord knows all about my circumstances and how I'm holding up. He will often open up little windows for me, just when I need them.

Are you feeling overwhelmed today? Find a resting place. Even if it's just fifteen minutes in a quiet little nook where nobody will notice you, it will make a difference in your day. Ask God to recharge your batteries for the tasks that await you. Remember that he knows what is facing you, and he will give you strength to get through it.

This day, Lord: I know I need times set apart from the press of demands, to refresh my spirit. Help me find a resting place to catch my breath today and refocus my attention on you. Amen.

Celebrating Real-Life Moments

Sometimes, being receptive to life's simple gifts means changing our focus from what has to get done to what is happening right now.

Years ago when I was singing with the Dallas Opera, I was working at Mobil during the day. Every evening I would sing from about six until midnight and then get up and go to work the next day. In the fall, we would perform three or four different operas. This required learning new music, attending numerous rehearsals, undergoing costume fittings. It took a great deal of time.

I remember quite vividly an experience I had one evening in the midst of one of our busiest cycles. We were in a chorus director's hotel room in downtown Dallas, way up on the twelfth floor. We were all dead tired and out of sorts. The week had been particularly exhausting. There was an ensemble of about twelve women who had to learn very difficult parts, in French. None of us was hitting the notes right, and the rehearsal was not going well. Frustration and fatigue were mounting.

Then the two men who were directing the rehearsal stopped us abruptly. They went over to the windows and pulled the curtains all the way back. We stared out into the moonlight over a panoramic view of the city, lit up in splendor. The guys turned off all the lights in the room except for one light over the piano. They sat down on the piano bench together, the room now in total silence. Then they began to play. For the next twenty minutes they serenaded us by singing Italian love songs. They really didn't sing all that well, but that didn't matter. The spirit of the moment was overwhelmingly lovely.

I remember feeling the fatigue drain out of me as I thought to myself, *THIS is real life. It is beautiful! Not just to the eye but to the ear—it is a feast. Thank you, Lord.*

There have been many times in my life when it seems that everything is in total chaos, and along will come something beautiful that arrests my attention. Suddenly the chaos doesn't seem so overwhelming anymore. Or I will be happily surprised by some little occurrence, such as a woman dragging a motley crew of unkempt kids into a waiting room, and I'm thinking, *Oh no, here we go,* and it turns out she's just wonderful with them, and it lifts my spirit.

I call these episodes "real life" moments. However small or incidental they might seem, they can have a powerful effect on us. Be on the watch for these moments that God will bring into your life. They will change your perspective from anxiety to gratitude. You'll know when you find yourself thinking, *Now THIS is real life. Thank you, Lord.*

This day, Lord: Open my eyes to "real life" moments that replace fatigue and worry with joy and gratitude. Amen.

The Joy of Now

Sometimes in the midst of rushing from one trip to the next I'll think, *I wish I had more time.* But then I think, *But my life might not be as rich as it is now if it weren't so demanding.* The surprises are all the more surprising because I'm in a place that I wouldn't necessarily have chosen. If I had set out to create the ideal schedule in my natural environment, it would probably look a lot different from the life I'm in now.

Having been in the business world by choice for so many years, I don't have as strong a sense of calling in my ministry to women as those who have always been ministry driven. Therefore when my resources start running thin, my tendency is to question why God has me here. I start feeling like I don't have a lot to offer.

These tend to be the very times when God will bring some affirmation to me that

I'm right where he wants me. In these "aha" moments, the Lord reminds me that he cares about that part of me that's feeling exhausted or bereft or needy or empty. I remember the time I was starting at Mobil, and it was pouring down rain, and I didn't want to go. I asked the Lord to give me something to laugh at. I pulled off the freeway to go to Long Beach, and sitting in the cab of a pickup truck next to me were two fully dressed clowns. It lifted my spirit for the whole day.

These "aha" moments have happened on planes, in arenas, at book signings. I remember a woman coming up to me and saying, "This book about the single life changed my life. It was the only thing I ever read that made me glad I was single. And I'm now married, and I wish there was something like this for married people!" Incidents like that are God's gifts to me. They stop me in my tracks and refocus me on the joy of *now*.

Take your fatigue and your questions to the Lord. Ask him to open your eyes to the joy of what he is doing in your life *right now*. You just never know what might happen next.

*This day, Lord: I need an "aha" moment.
Lift my spirit with a reminder of how
you are at work in my life right now, in
the midst of whatever struggles and
challenges I face. Amen.*

Tomorrow's life is too late. Live today.

—Marcus Valerius Martialis

I will praise you as long as I live, and in your

name I will lift up my hands.

—Psalm 63:4

Get Real

$\mathcal{I}$ heard Joni Tada recount the story of how she dove into Chesapeake Bay and became paralyzed. Later, when reading the Word of God, she came upon Paul's observation in Romans 5 that "suffering brings about patience." She thought to herself, *The nerve of the Bible to tell me that suffering brings about patience—with the degree of my paralysis, which I have now been enduring for three decades!*

I loved her honesty. Many of us are not very good at it. We expend a lot of energy trying to fit the profile we think others want to see. This isolates us from the support that others can provide. But it also keeps others from seeing the most profound work of God in our lives. Because Joni Tada does not hide her struggles, we are deeply moved by her grip on God's grace in the midst of excruciating circumstances.

I believe the secret in ministering to others is honesty about our lives. We have holes; we're human. Paul provides a wonderful image for this reality: we are treasures in jars of clay. God speaks to others through what he does in our lives.

When I speak at Women of Faith events and see the responses of all the women who come, I wonder if they are having difficulty finding their place in church. It seems such a tremendous release for them to come to these events and let it all hang out. They can come with their buddies; they can dress the way they want to; they can have a wonderful time of worship and singing and laughing and crying and feeling. When they leave, they don't have to sign their name to anything or get on somebody's list to do something. They just get to come and be who they are—no strings attached.

Do you want more of God, more of his transforming work in your life? Do you want more from your relationships? Ask God for the courage to be honest about what's really going on in your life. Be who you are in Christ. Get real!

This day, Lord: Shine through me in those very places where I am most likely to feel discouragement and failure. Help me remember that others will be drawn to you not by my accomplishment but by your grace. Amen.

Hands off the Controls

This year I am focusing on "revolutionary freedom," which I think is wonderful for me. I am probably the queen of those who hate legalism. In some ways women are especially susceptible to legalism, because it supports their inbred desire to control circumstances, their husbands, their kids' lives, themselves.

When Jesus comes into my life, when he dies for me, he sets me free from the tyranny of legalism. But this is a freedom I have to embrace—I won't experience it if I continue in bondage to my need for control.

I love reading in Hebrews, my favorite book, about all that we are offered in Jesus Christ—in his superior life, in his superior death, in his superior priesthood. Because of his sacrifice, we no longer live under the law. We are privileged to be in a new covenant with God. It is a covenant of grace. But some women continue in bondage, not realizing that they are inadvertently still choosing to live under the law. They don't know that God in his grace became poor—Scripture says he became poverty-stricken—so that they can be rich and live free and abundant lives.

When I think about these truths, I am filled with a desire to tell others. I've learned these lessons the hard way. I know how much we need them. So for me, this news is worth telling. It's worth leaving home and going through endless airports and getting up on stage in front of thousands of women to proclaim, "You cannot fix it. It is not fixable by a human being. God has to fix it. Let it go!"

Letting go is scary. But when you finally do it, God will fill your life with his own transcendent riches. It's a lesson you will have to learn over and over again. Like peace, freedom from legalism has to be re-won every day. You don't get it once and for all. But this means that each day, you have a fresh chance to get out from under the law. Take your hands off the controls; God will lift you to another place of living: the realm of grace.

This day, Lord: Help me let go of trying to control my life. Set me free to trust in your sovereign grace in my life. Amen.

Beauty and Coming Glory

When I was in art school, I studied the treasures of Egypt. How I loved that! By now I've been to many museums around the world, and I've seen these treasures with my own eyes. I know firsthand how absolutely mesmerizing they are.

When I think of beauty, I think of Hebrews 11, the faith chapter, where all those heroic guys like Gideon are mentioned. Moses appears in this hall of fame. He is commended for having considered disgrace for the sake of Christ to be of greater value than all the treasures of Egypt. He was looking ahead to his reward.

This passage comes to my mind whenever I hear or see something that is really beautiful. I think, *God is even greater than this glimpse of beauty he has given you— he is more faithful, he is more perfect, he is more abiding, he is more constant, he is more dazzling than this.* That has been a big help to me during the years. It's a foretaste of what is to come. What we get glimpses of now is terrific—but just think of what's down the road!

This day, Lord: Instill in me a fresh awareness of your glory through the beauty that is all around me.

Sing the glory of his name;

make his praise glorious!

—Psalm 66:2

When You Just Don't Want To

When I'm facing something I just don't want to do, I will sometimes pray, "Lord, to the degree that I don't want to do it, please bless it." If it's something I *really* don't want to do, then the blessing is just overwhelming. This has happened to me many times. The Lord will say to me, "You ain't seen nothin' yet—I'm gonna come in there like a flood. This is going to be so much fun. You're going to have your joy restored, so just shut up and sit down."

This "I don't want to" prayer helps me confess that my heart is not in it. It opens the way for God to do something surprising. More often than not, he will do something really cool! I'll think, *Yes—that's just what I needed, and I didn't even know it!*

I'm a take-charge person, so I usually have my own thing worked out well in advance. I usually feel pretty good about how I plan things, and I tend not to like sudden changes. When I read about how his ways are not my ways, and how his thoughts are higher than mine, I think, *Well, shoot, Lord—I know my ways! I've got* 'em all worked out here, thank you very much. Then you come in with this thing that looks half-baked, and you're telling me I've got to go that *direction*.

Almost always, before we're even halfway down the road in God's direction instead of mine, I start realizing, *Oh my gosh, this is so much better!* But I didn't want it, and I didn't feel it, so I have to pray, "To the degree that I don't want to do this, please bless it." That's about eighty to ninety per-cent of the time. It's kind of a reverse psy-chology thing, but it works for me. It's my way of being really honest with the Lord. He just comes in and tackles it, and he changes me as well as the circumstances.

Are you facing something that makes you feel faint of heart? You don't have to muster up the strength on your own. Just confess your unwillingness to God. Ask him to bless your efforts according to his pur-poses, not yours. Then take the next step, and watch what God does.

This day, Lord: In the challenges I wish I didn't have to face, strengthen me despite my reluctance. Bless these circumstances according to your purposes, and give me a grateful heart for how you will work through them. Amen.

O to grace how great a debtor
Daily I'm constrained to be!
Let Thy goodness like a fetter
Bind my wand'ring heart to Thee;
Prone to wander—Lord, I feel it—
Prone to leave the God I love;
Here's my heart—O take and seal it,
Seal it for Thy courts above.

—ROBERT ROBINSON

Be strong and take heart,

All you who hope in the LORD.

—PSALM 31:24

He gives us more grace. That

is why Scripture says:

"God opposes the proud

but gives grace to the humble."

Submit yourselves, then, to God.

Resist the devil, and he will flee

from you. Come near to God and

he will come near to you.

—JAMES 4:6–8

Wherever You Go, There He Is

The book of Romans means the world to me—the truth that we don't live anymore under condemnation; we are completely loved by the Lord. There isn't anything that can make us step outside that love. Then when you get to Romans 8:28—about everything working together for good. When I'm praying about something at my end of the line, the Lord is working on something at the other end of the line. It will be perfect; it will work out well; it will be a wonderful revelation of his ability to meet me exactly where I am. I don't have to clean up my act; I don't have to be different; I don't have to do anything differently. He will meet me in my reality.

Those verses are just great. I think, too, that the truth of grace is probably the thing that has changed my life the most and taken me out of a legalistic lifestyle I had when I was young and trying to get everybody to "shape up." He loved me in spite of myself, and he continues to. That is very healing and very enriching. It makes all the difference in how I face today.

I will often pray these words: "It's just you and me, Lord." Being single, I have faced countless problems—money crisis, surgery, car breakdown, delay on arriving on time for some commitment. I pray, "Lord, you've never let me down yet." I know he will help me do the next thing, whatever that will be.

This day, Lord: Meet me in the realities of my life. Remind me that you are always present with me. Amen.

Do not be afraid or discouraged, for the Lord God, my God, is with you.

—1 Chronicles 28:20

Pay Attention

*I*f I had just one piece of advice to give you so you can go forth this week and live in the moment, I would say, "Practice mindfulness."

The Lord has said that if we abide in him, he will abide in us. Now, what does "abide" really mean? I think it means kind of snuggle in there—get in there and relax and enjoy and have a cup of tea. I tell myself, *Okay, Luci, you've got it clear in your mind; now go and practice it!* Whether it's a lovely day or a challenging day, he has made it, and he is in charge of it. Being mindful of that helps me refocus. Instead of worrying about whatever else is supposed to be happening, I'll concentrate on being present in everything this day and capitalizing on whatever happens. He has not given me the spirit of fear, but of a sound mind. He will help me with whatever it is I'm focusing my mind on. This helps me live now instead of putting off living.

Sure, there are some things we can't have now, but we won't have *anything* now if we're always waiting for something to get better or more organized or less chaotic, or to occur with fewer interruptions. I deal constantly with interruptions, and I have to say to myself, *Luci, this is part of God's teaching you. Take it as it comes. Pay attention to this.*

Pay attention and let God surprise you. Enjoy now. Feel now. Learn now. Love now. Live now.

This day, Lord: I want to abide in you. I want to be mindful of what you are doing in my life. Teach me to pay attention. Let me live to the fullest today. Amen.

Hold every moment sacred. Give each clarity and meaning, each the weight of thine awareness, each its true and due fulfillment.

—THOMAS MANN

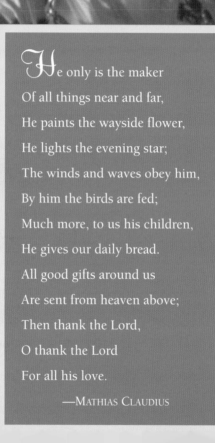

He only is the maker
Of all things near and far,
He paints the wayside flower,
He lights the evening star;
The winds and waves obey him,
By him the birds are fed;
Much more, to us his children,
He gives our daily bread.
All good gifts around us
Are sent from heaven above;
Then thank the Lord,
O thank the Lord
For all his love.

—Mathias Claudius